THE PLAYFUL
PINUP:
SHOWCASING THE ART OF
MAXWELL H. JOHNSON

First published in 2018 by Max Makes Photos Publishing.
Printed by CreateSpace.

Printed in the United States of America

ISBN-13: 978-0692061954
ISBN-10: 0692061959

THE PLAYFUL PINUP:

SHOWCASING THE ART OF
MAXWELL H. JOHNSON

Author: Kristin E. Johnson
Photographer: Maxwell H. Johnson

#PlayfulPinup

TABLE OF CONTENTS

ABOUT THE ARTIST

Maxwell H. Johnson is a photographer, artist, and graphic designer living in San Jose, California. He has been creating pinup art since 2007.

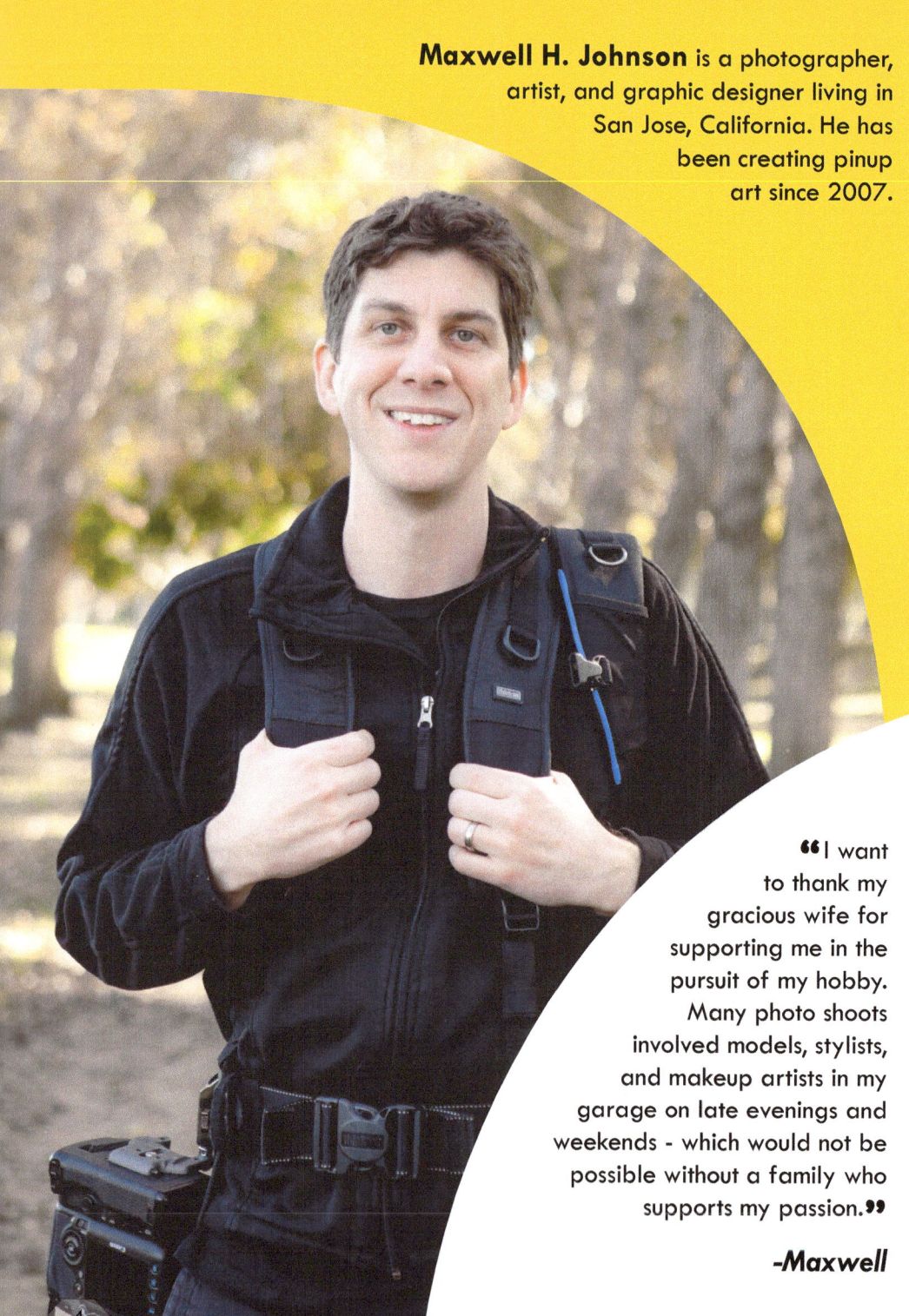

"I want to thank my gracious wife for supporting me in the pursuit of my hobby. Many photo shoots involved models, stylists, and makeup artists in my garage on late evenings and weekends - which would not be possible without a family who supports my passion.**"**

-Maxwell

FROM THE ARTIST

I've been doing photography of all types since high school, but it was not until 2007 that I discovered a penchant for pinup photography in particular. I immediately fell in love. **It is a style that combines sexiness and silliness in a bright, happy, occasionally polka-dotted package.**

There is something magical about the pinup genre. It speaks of an era where the rigid male-dominated power structures were just beginning to erode. There was a shift in the tone of how women were being depicted. **Outlandish costumes not withstanding, they began to be shown as assertive, fun-loving, and conscious of women's own sexuality.**

In my own work, I try to convey a mood of playful flirtation and self-aware satire. I like my photos to be sexy, but I strive to make them in such a way that "sexy" is not the first adjective that comes to mind. I'm hoping for something more like... delightful.

As a photographer, I love working with other people. Models, makeup artists, hair stylists, wardrobe experts: these are the collaborators and conspirators whose talents I rely on.

As you look through the vintage, holiday, military/ patriotic, and eclectic themed photos in this book, **I hope that you enjoy my work and appreciate the artistry of the people who were an integral behind-the- scenes part of making these pinups come to life.**

-Maxwell

QUICK FACTS

Name:
Maxwell H. Johnson

Age:
Born in 1982

Who Inspires You:
Gil Elvgren, Robert Alvarado

Pet:
A cat named Skittles

VINTAGE STYLE PINUPS

50'S RETRO, BOUDOIR, CORSET, PLAYING CARDS, WEATHERED, LINGERIE, FUR COAT.

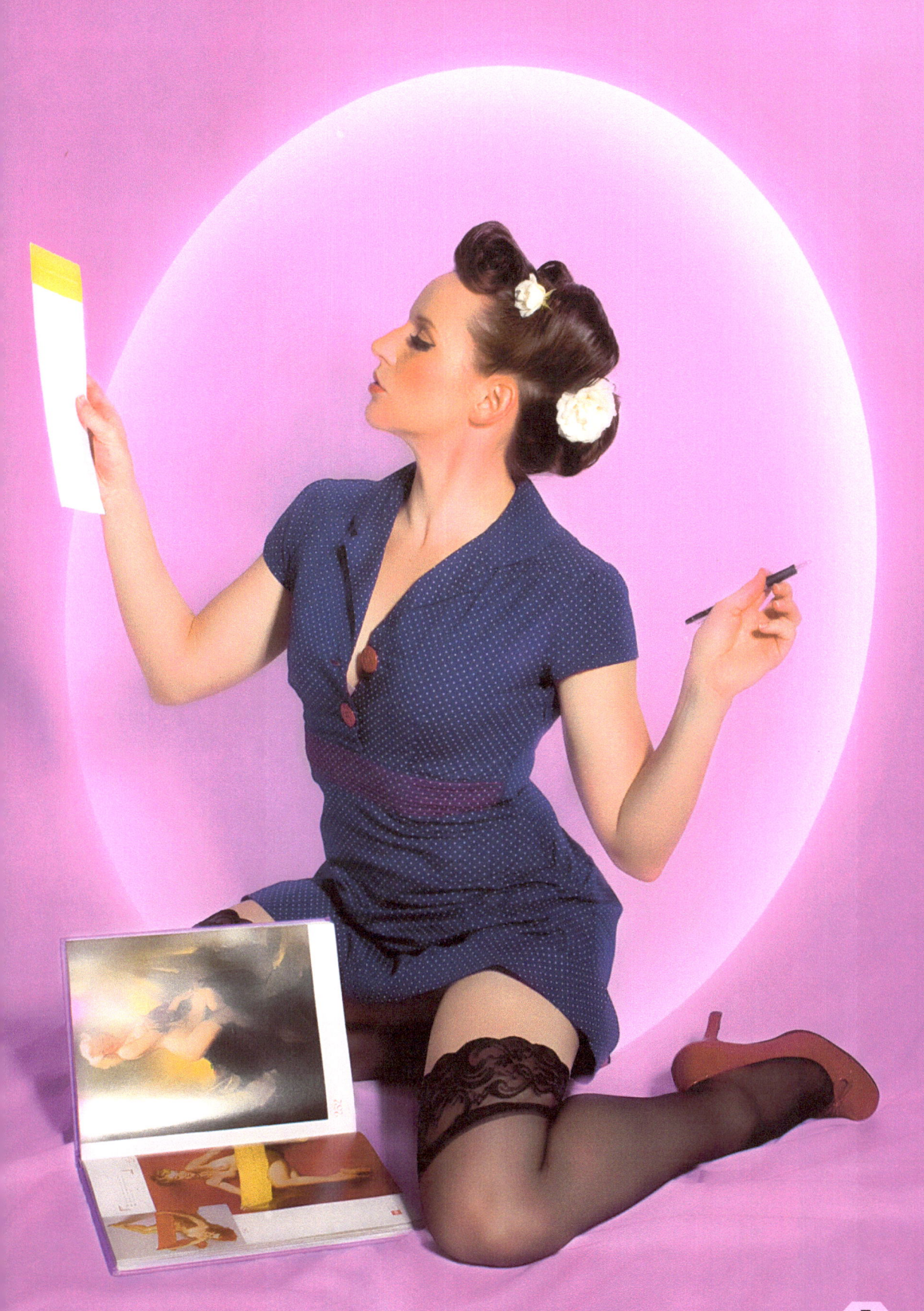

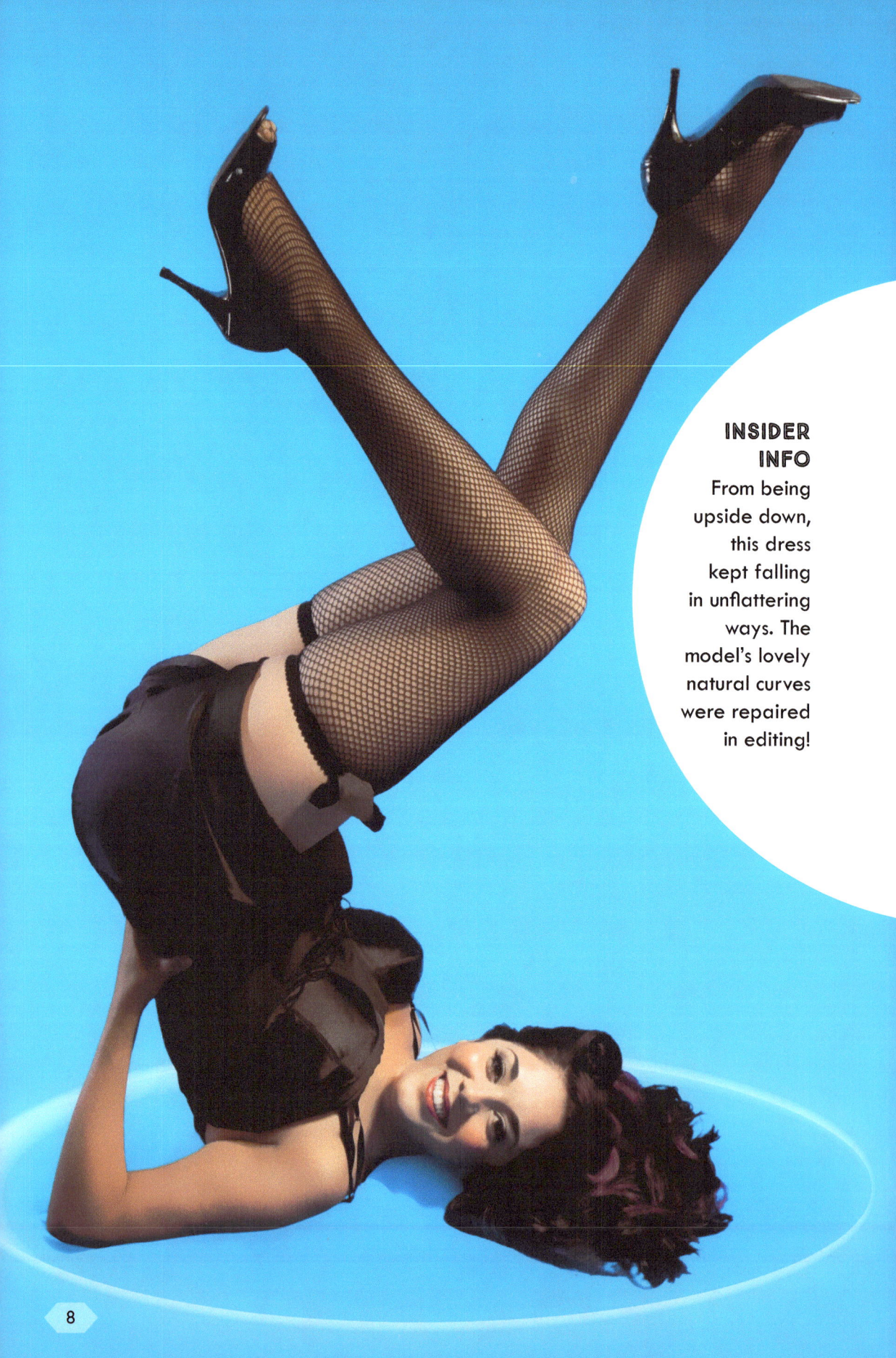

INSIDER INFO
From being upside down, this dress kept falling in unflattering ways. The model's lovely natural curves were repaired in editing!

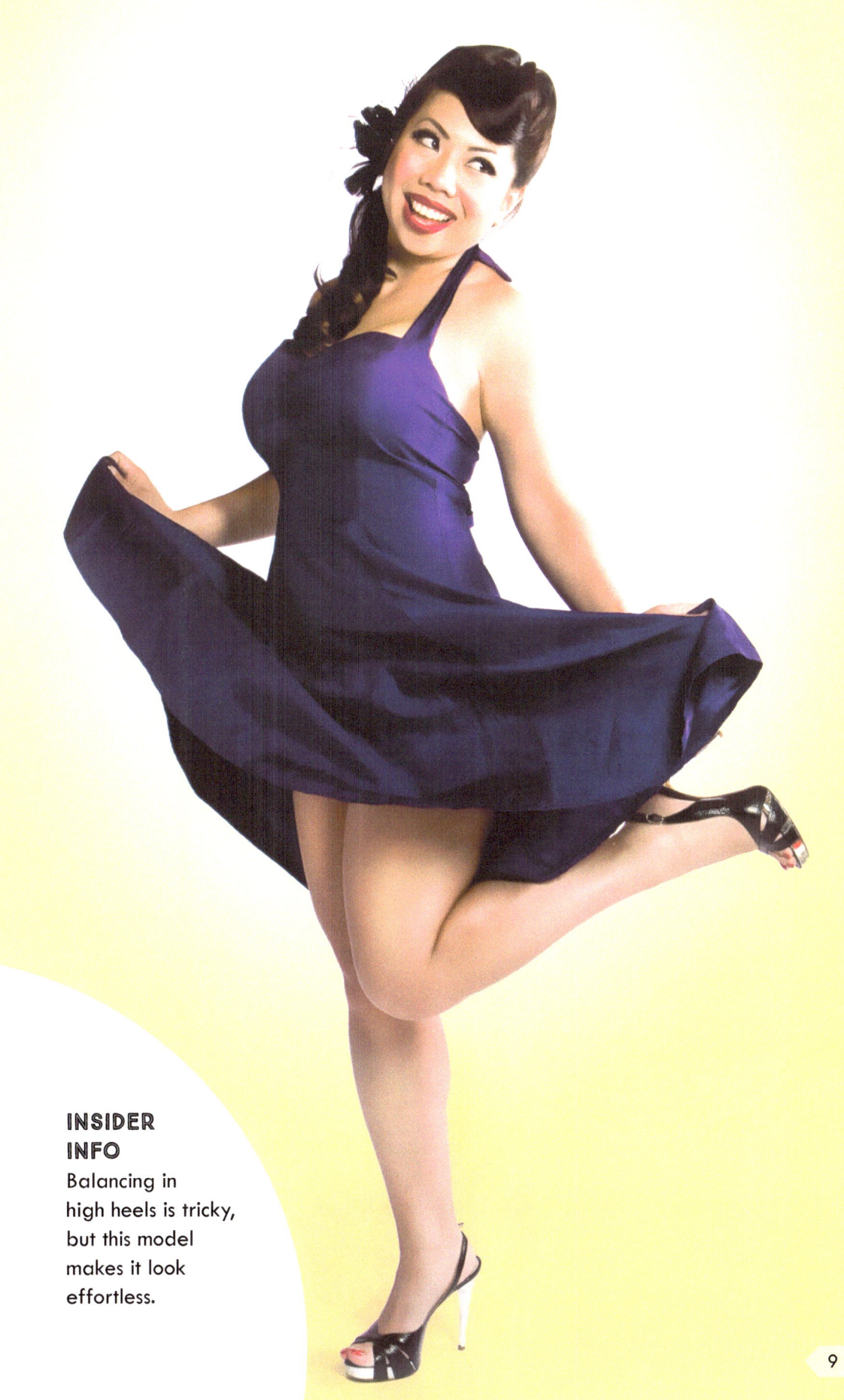

INSIDER INFO
Balancing in high heels is tricky, but this model makes it look effortless.

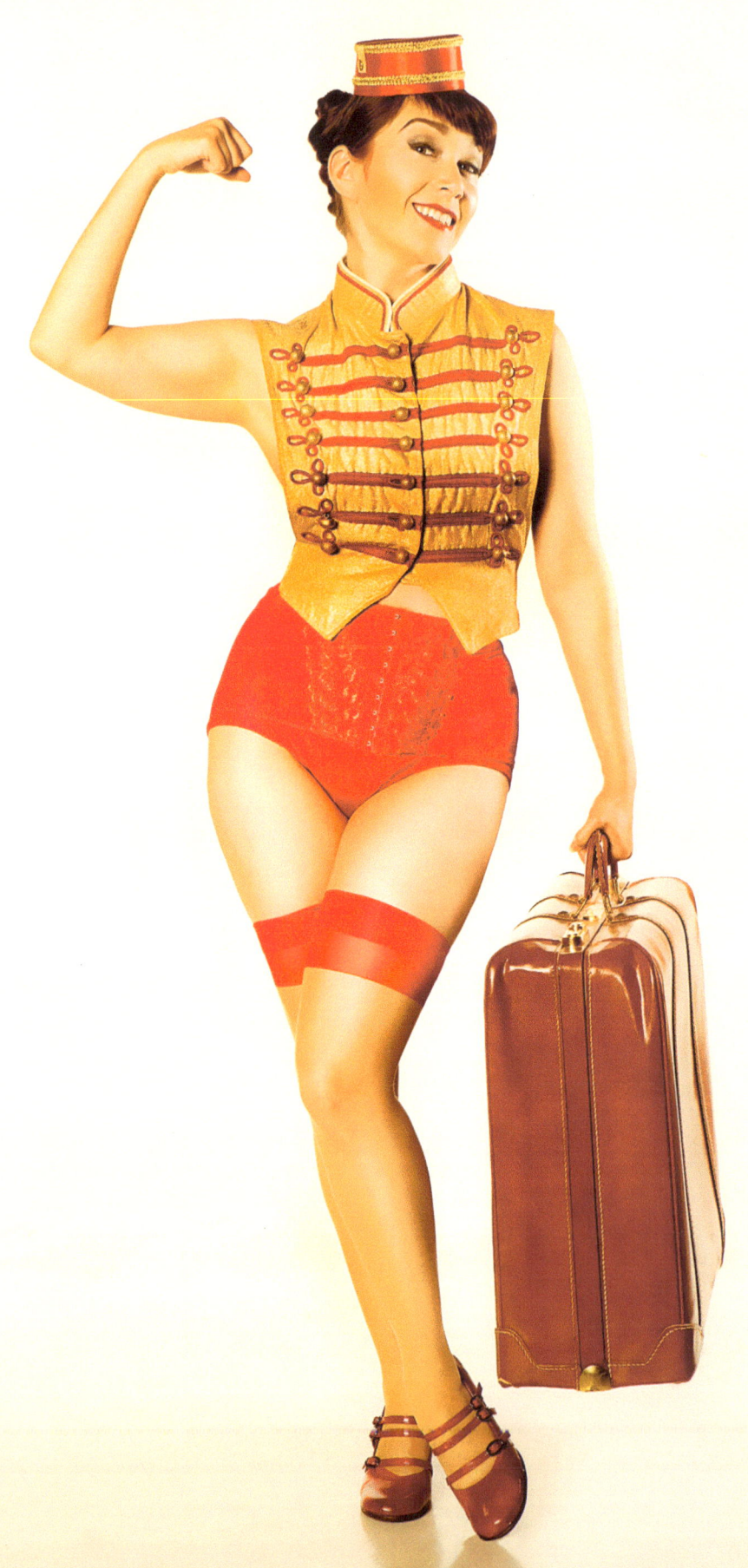

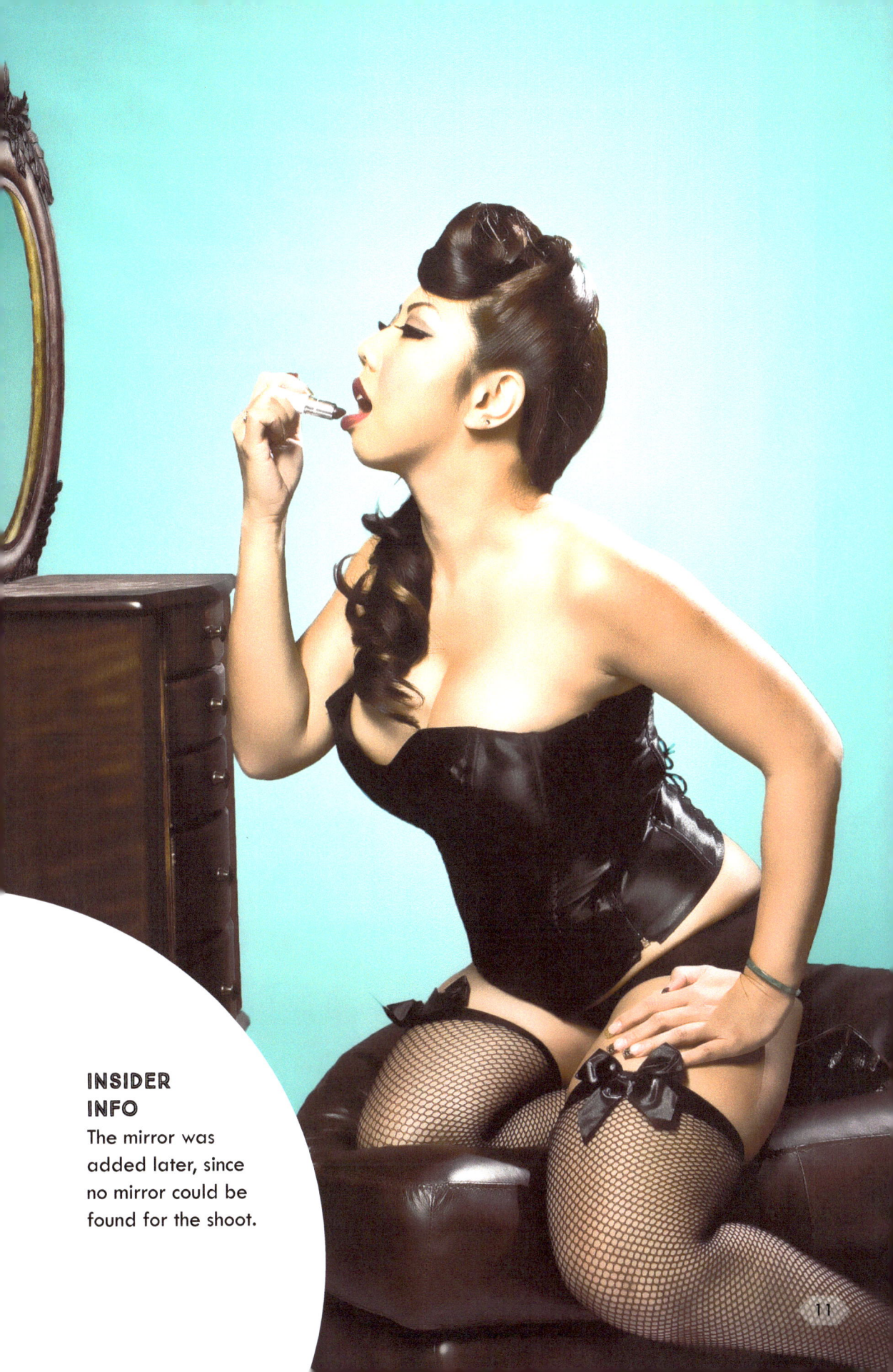

INSIDER INFO

The mirror was added later, since no mirror could be found for the shoot.

BEHIND THE SCENES

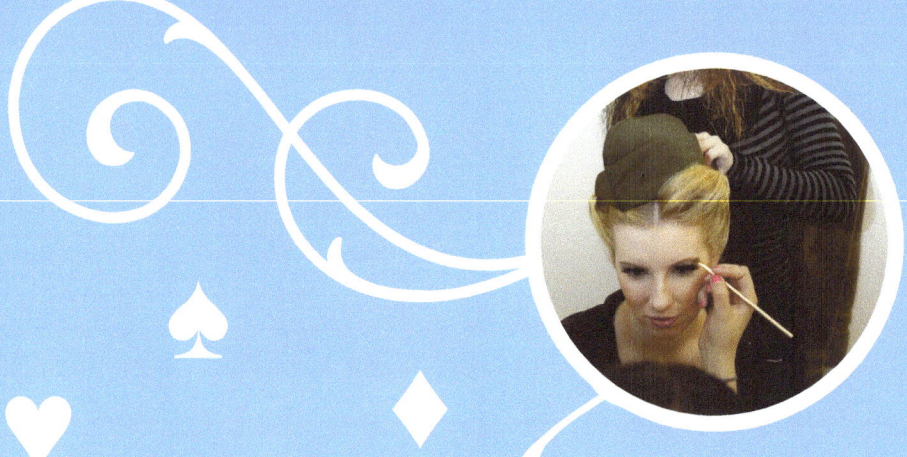

INSPIRATION
Classic pinup styling.

HAIR AND MAKEUP
Hours of careful hair styling and make-up were an essential part of preparation for this photo shoot.

BACKGROUND
A simple white backdrop was used - wrinkles on the floor were edited out in post-production.

PLAYING CARDS
The added playing-card frames help give this series a more authentic feel.

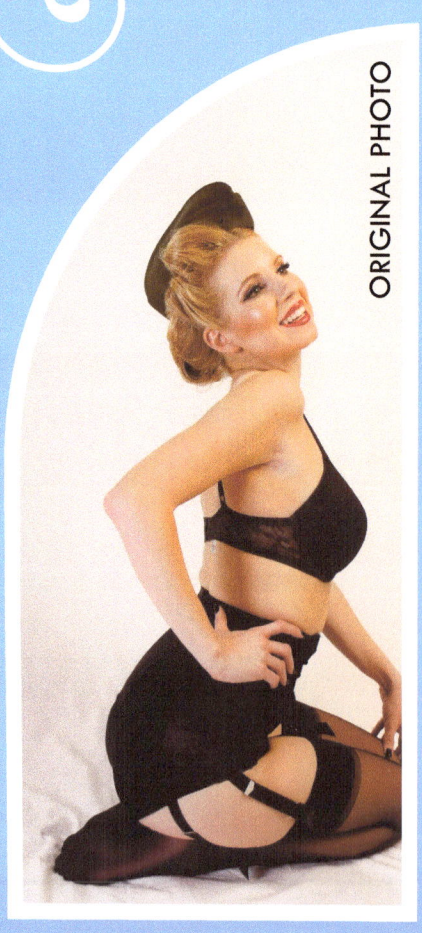

ORIGINAL PHOTO

9 ♣

♣ 6

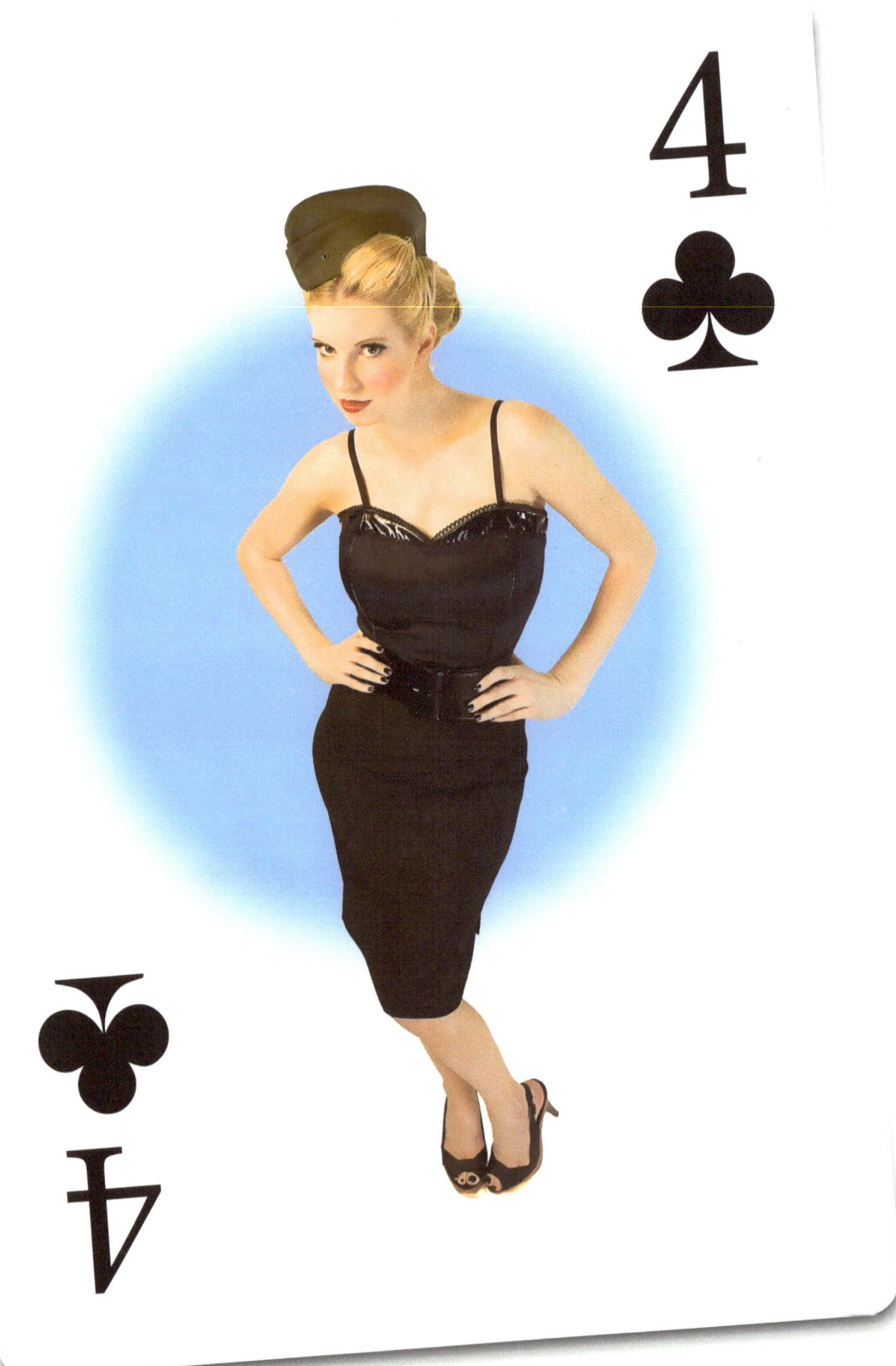

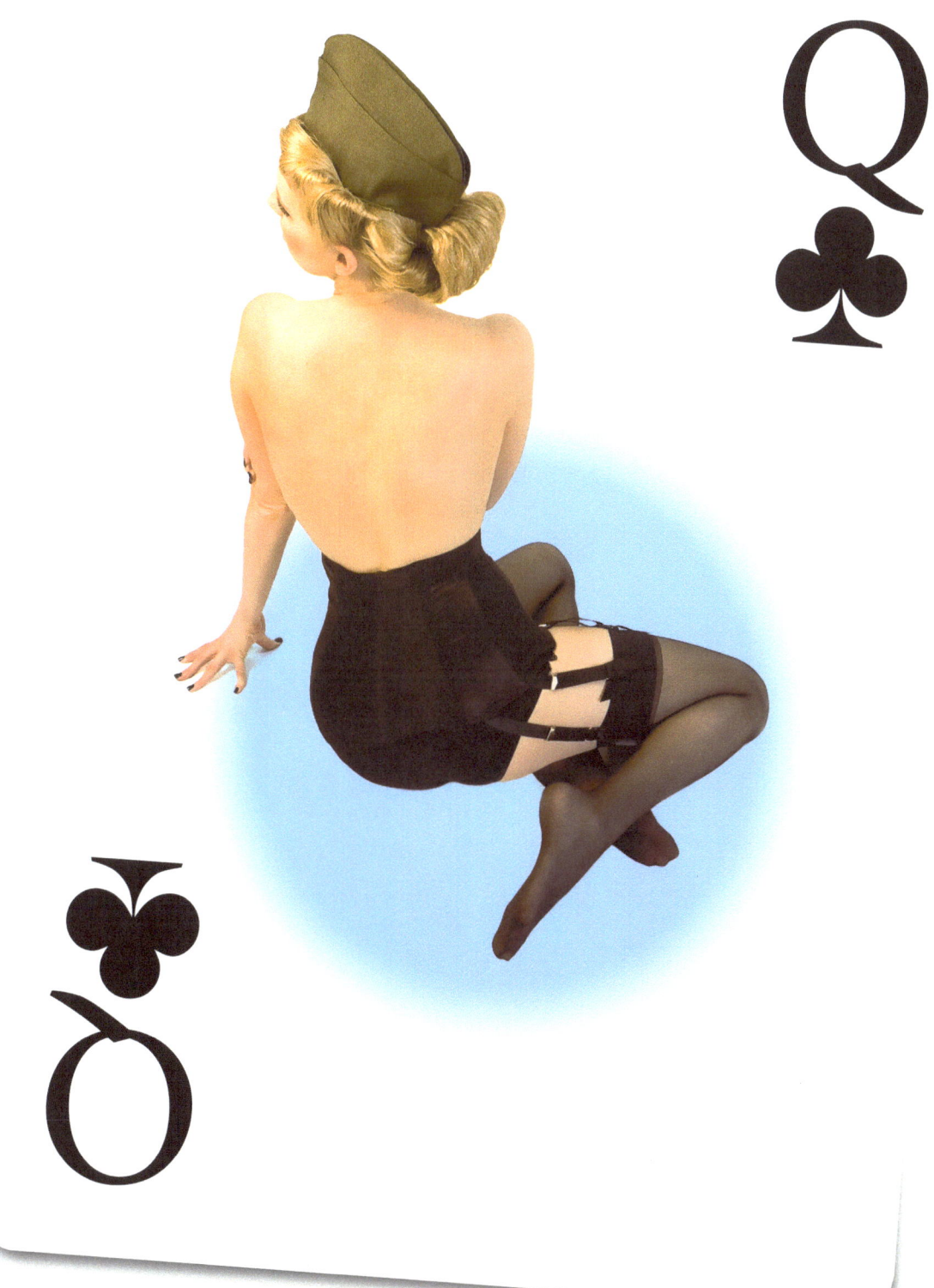

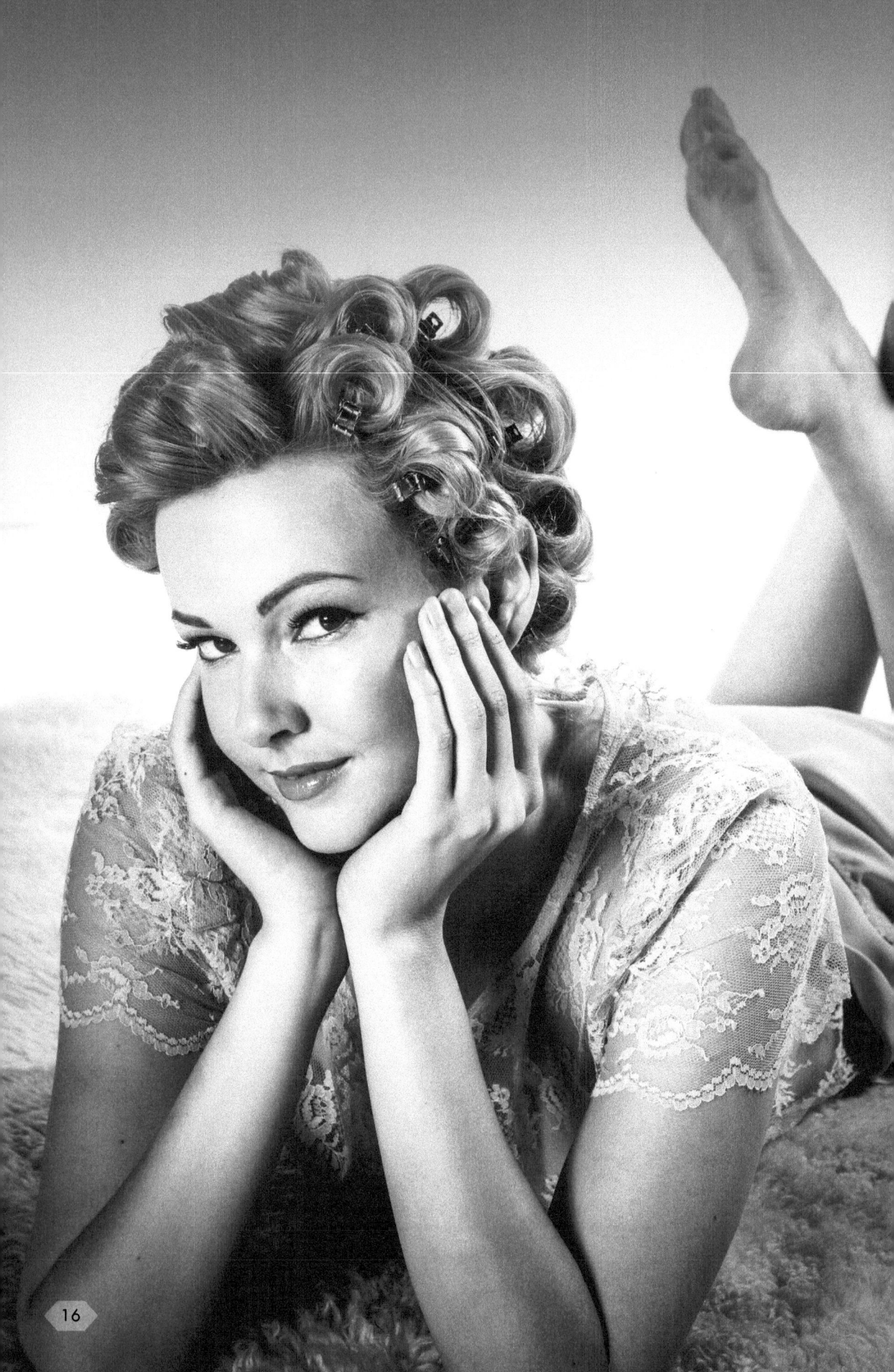

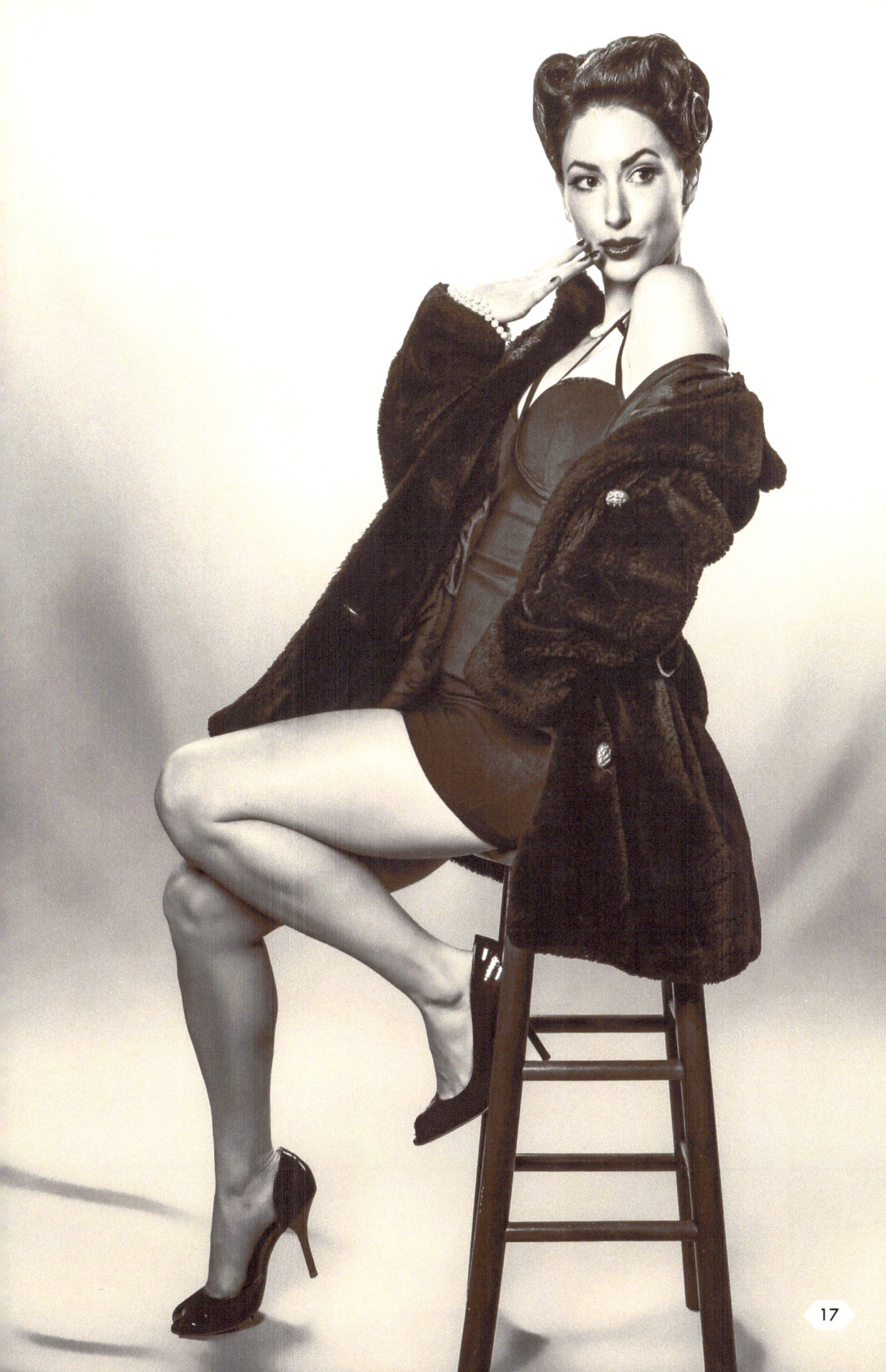

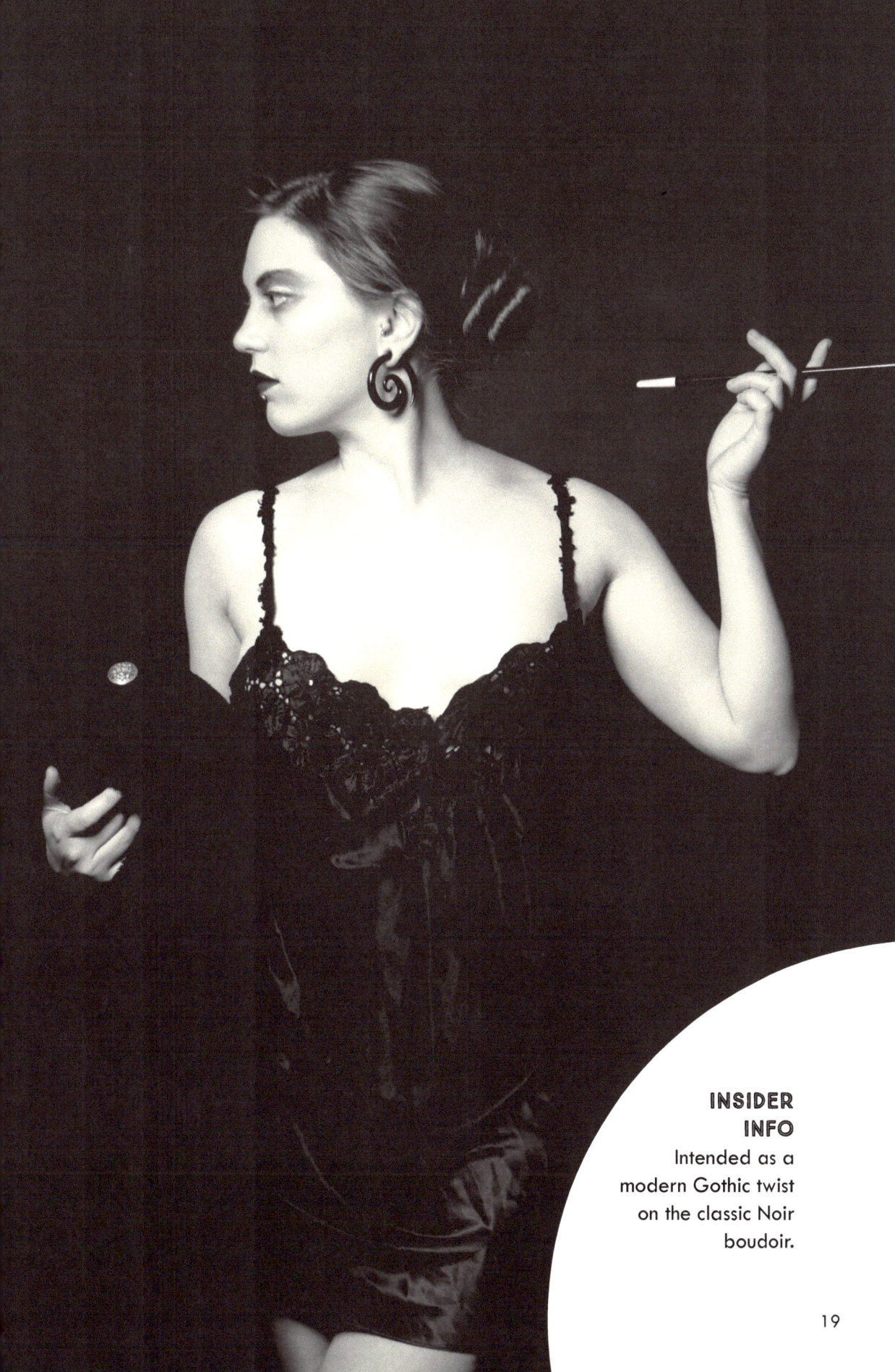

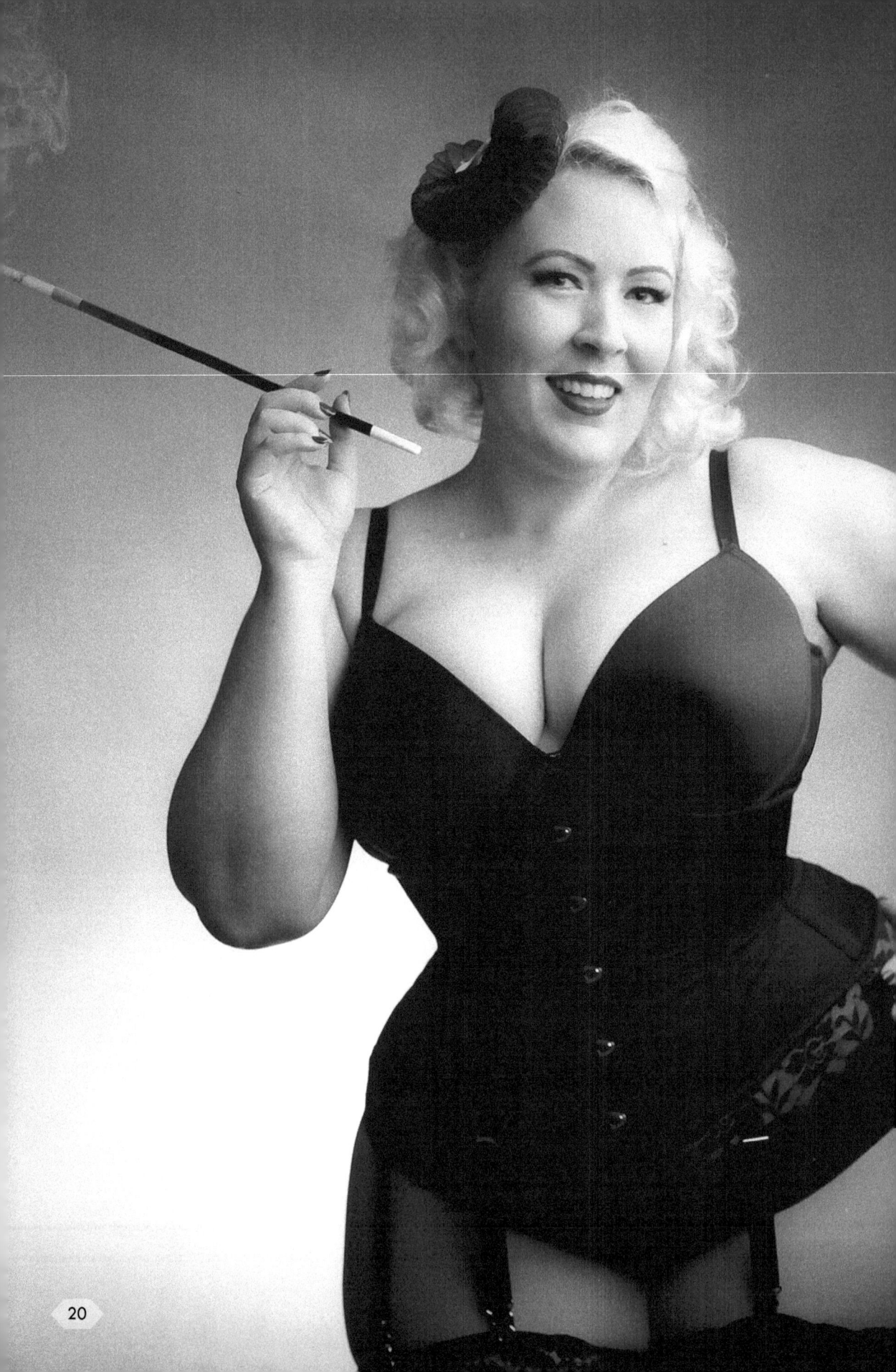

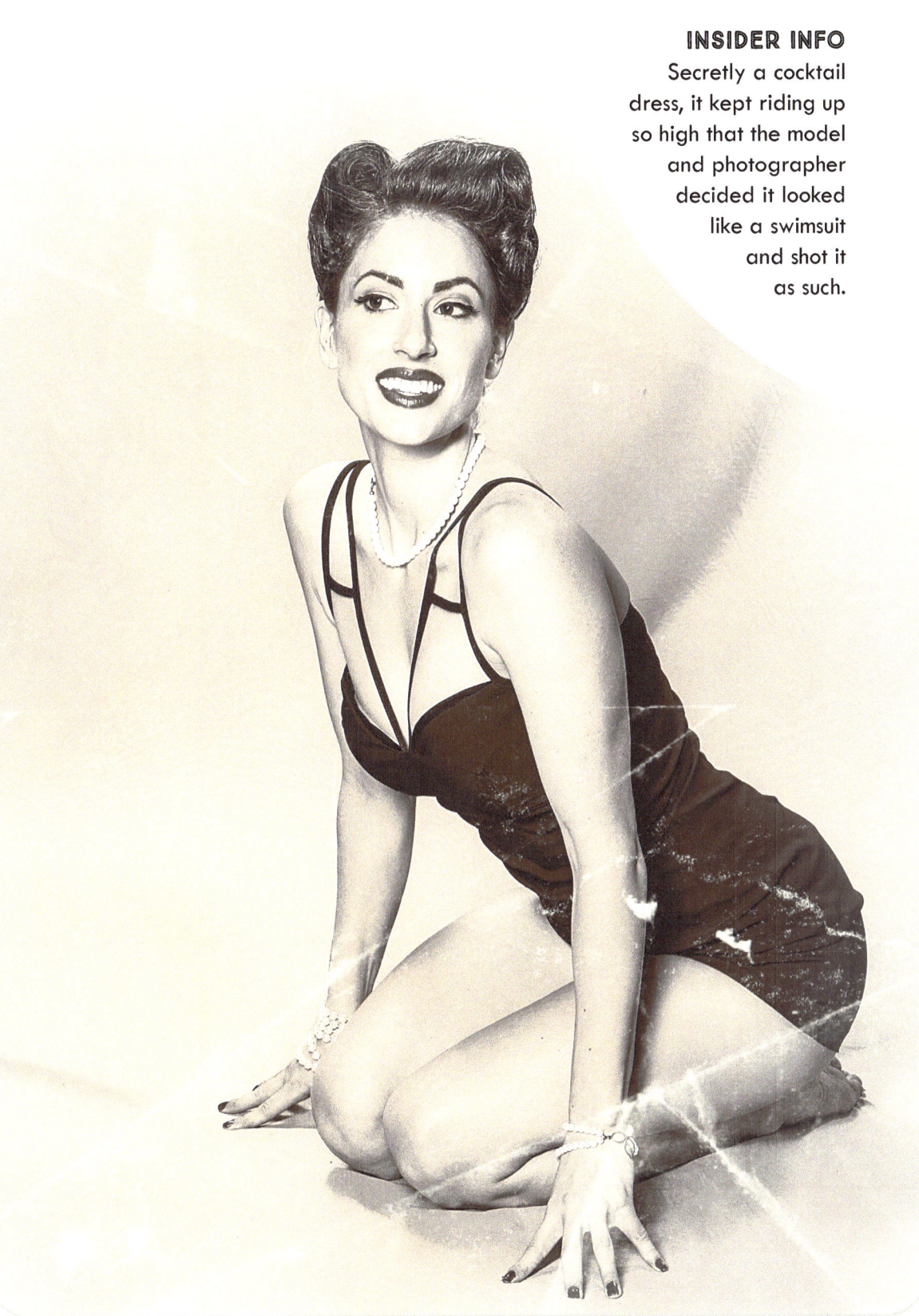

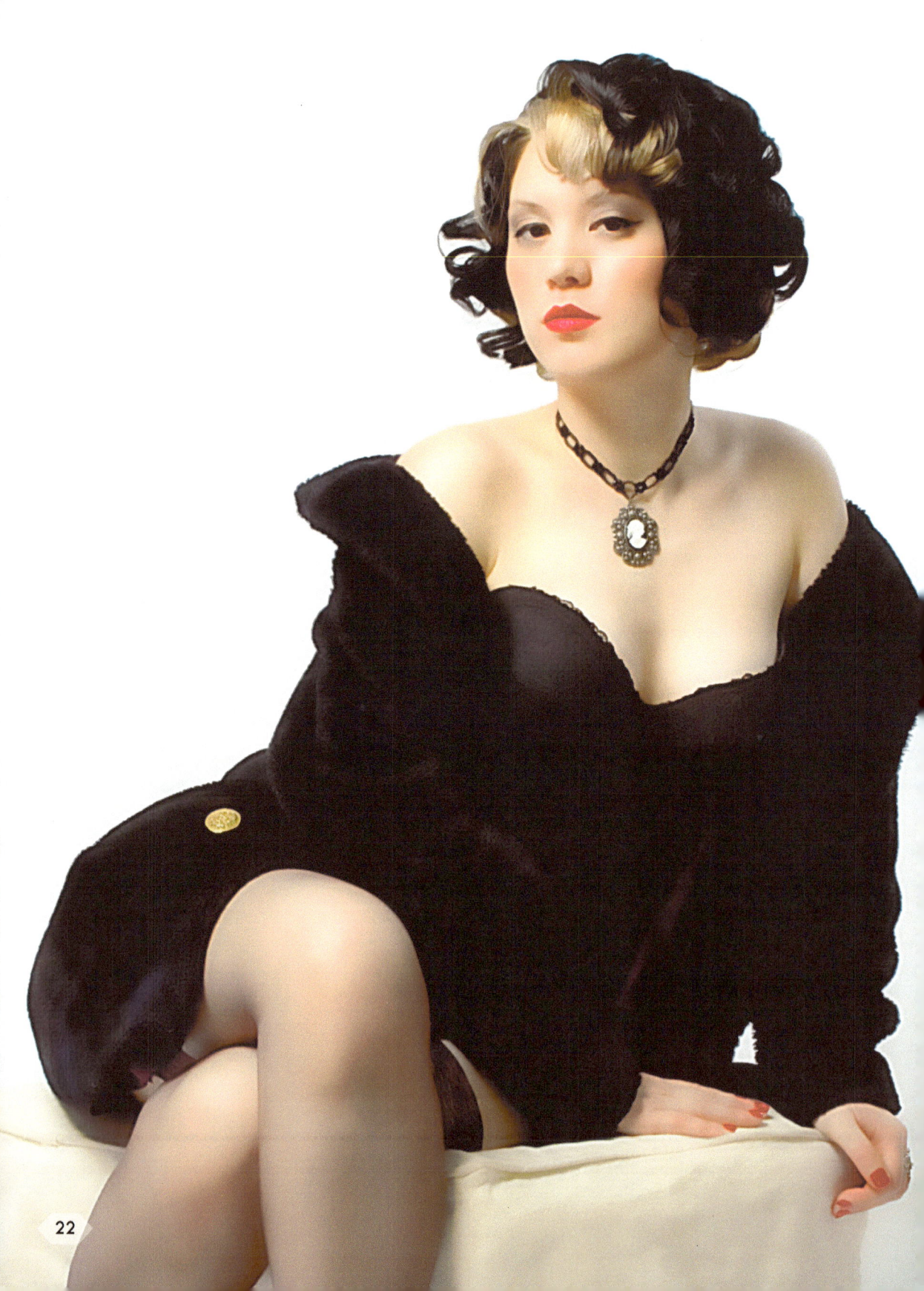

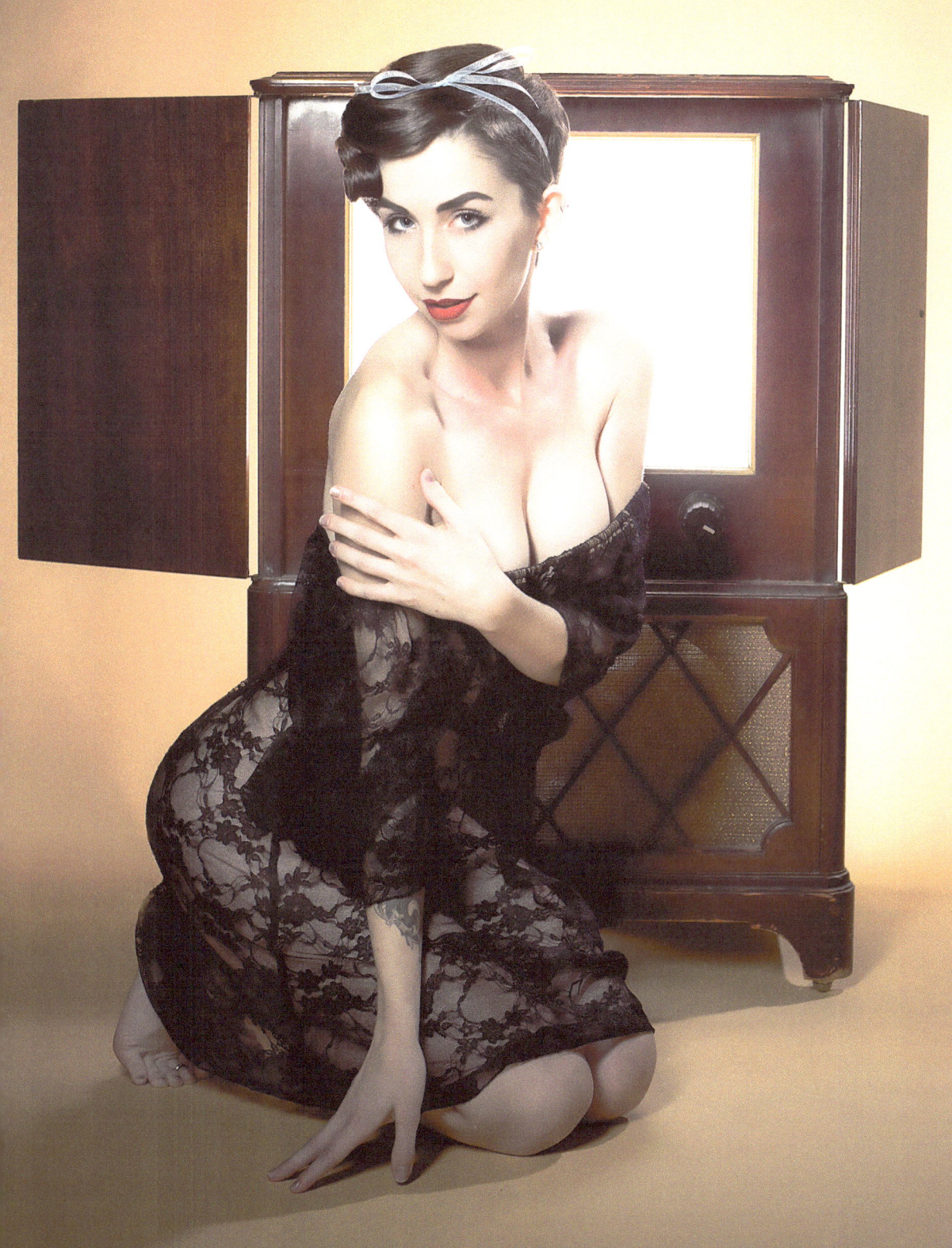

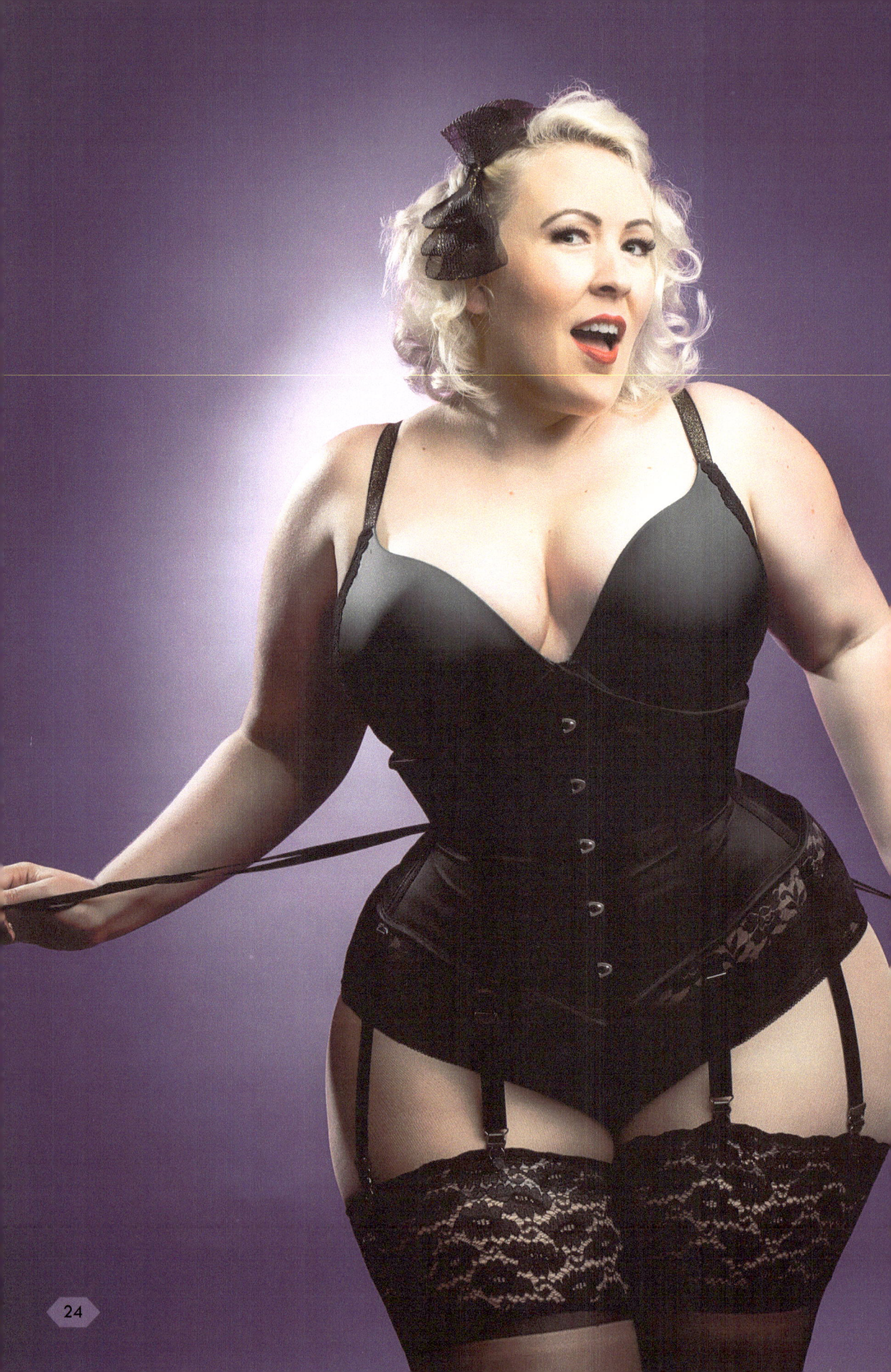

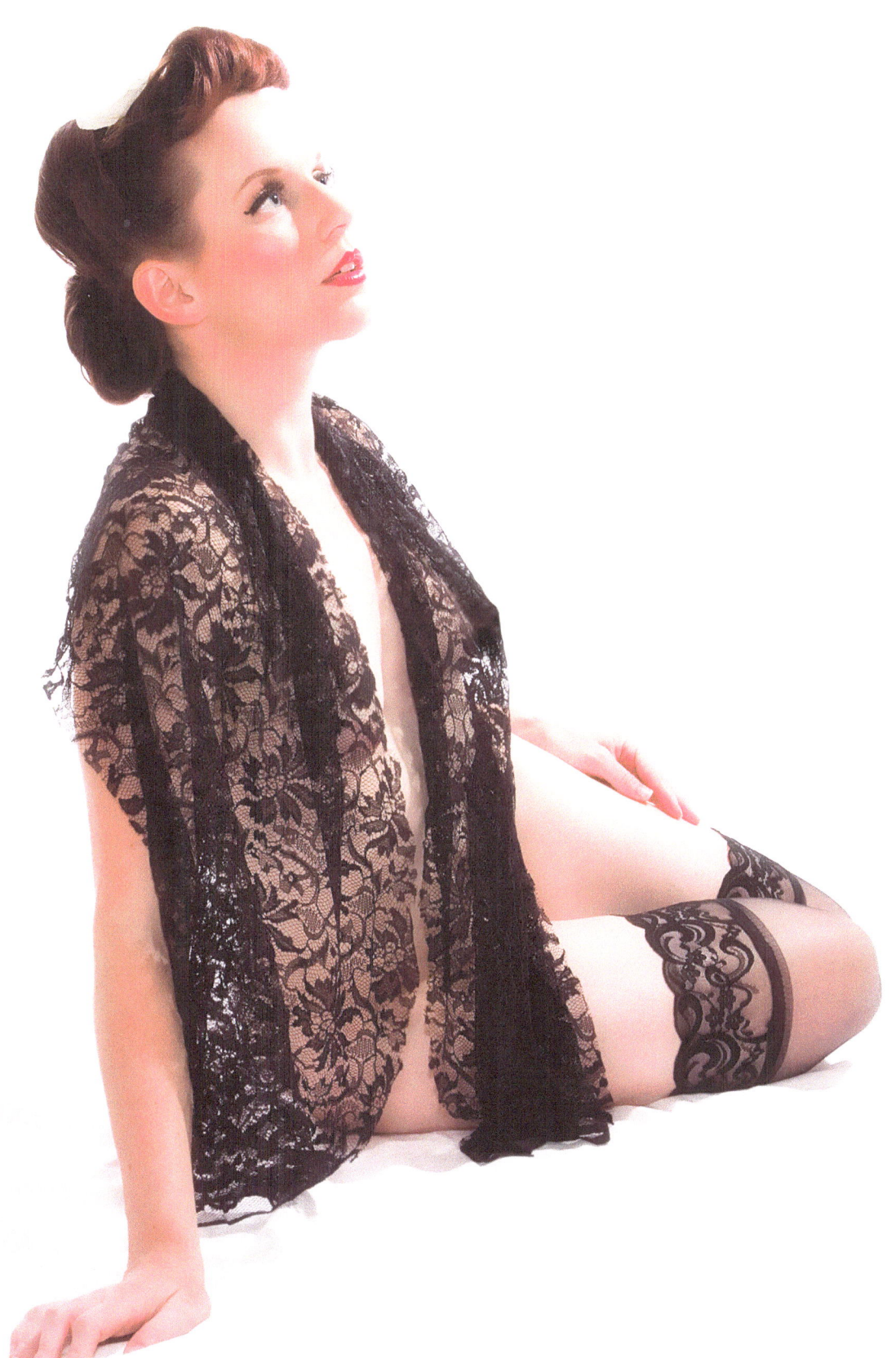

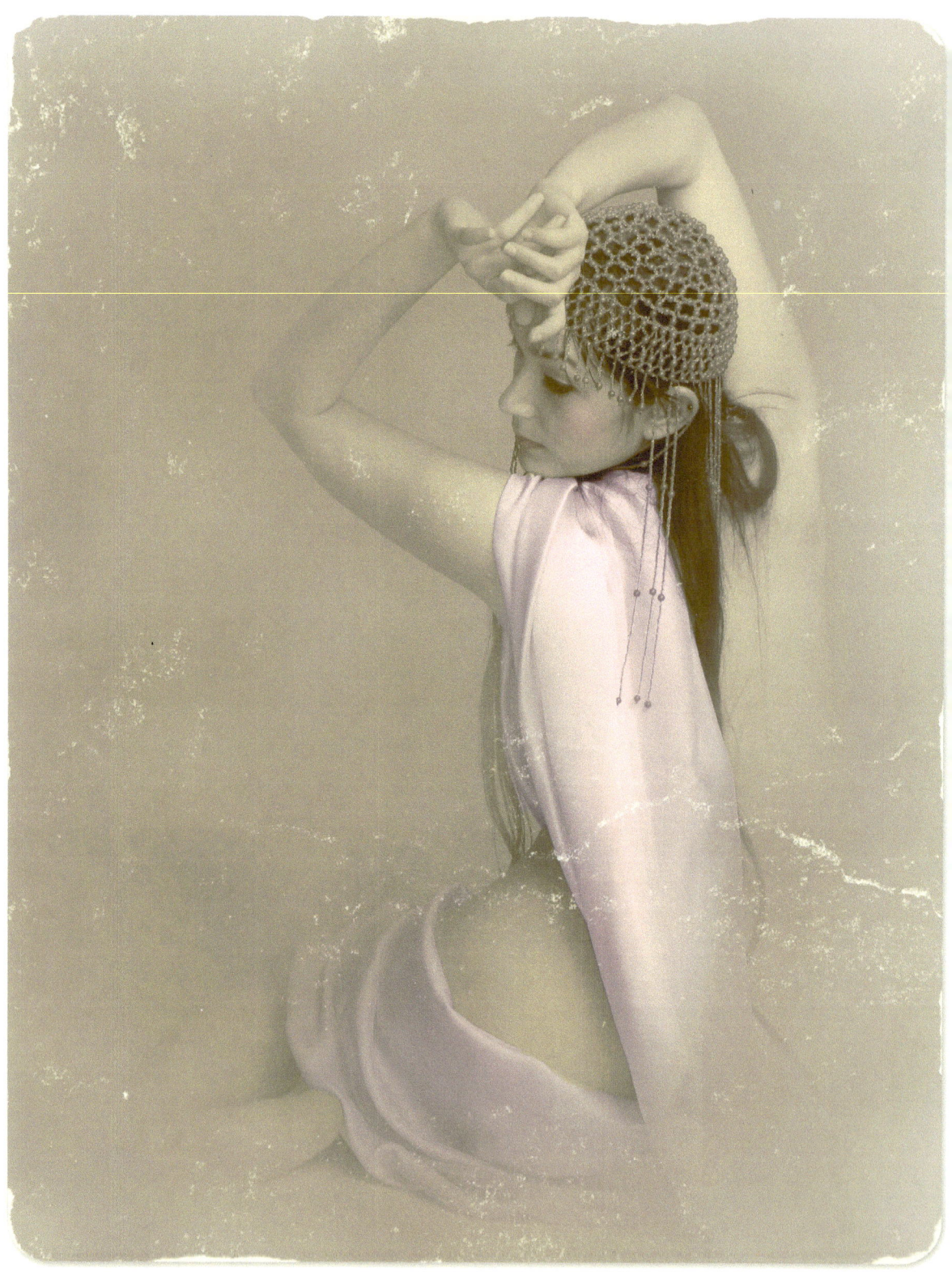

INSPIRATION

Inspired by antique glass-plate negatives in black and white that were recolored by hand with ink.

STYLING

Sometimes the simplest 'clothing' can still be effective for a pinup. This is literally a piece of draped satin fabric.

PROCESSING

The deeply weathered details were carefully added in editing, which ads a more authentic vintage look to the final design.

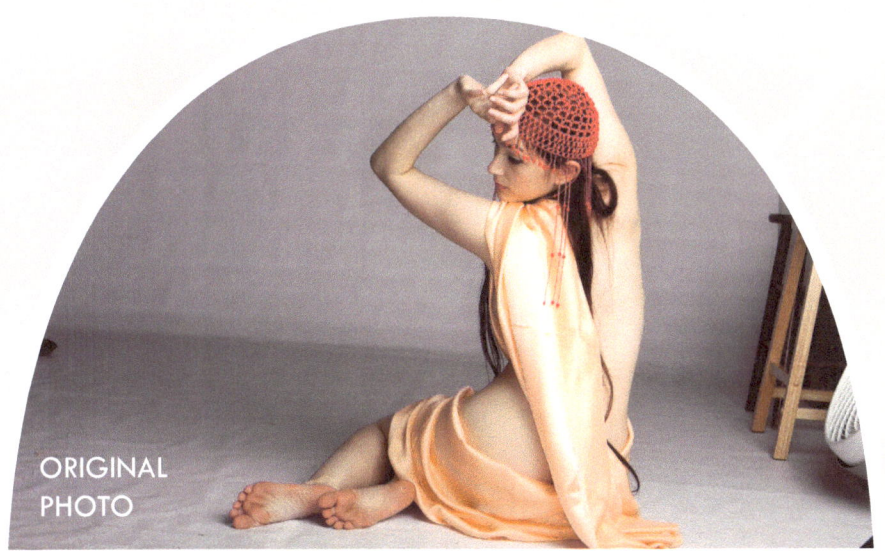

ORIGINAL
PHOTO

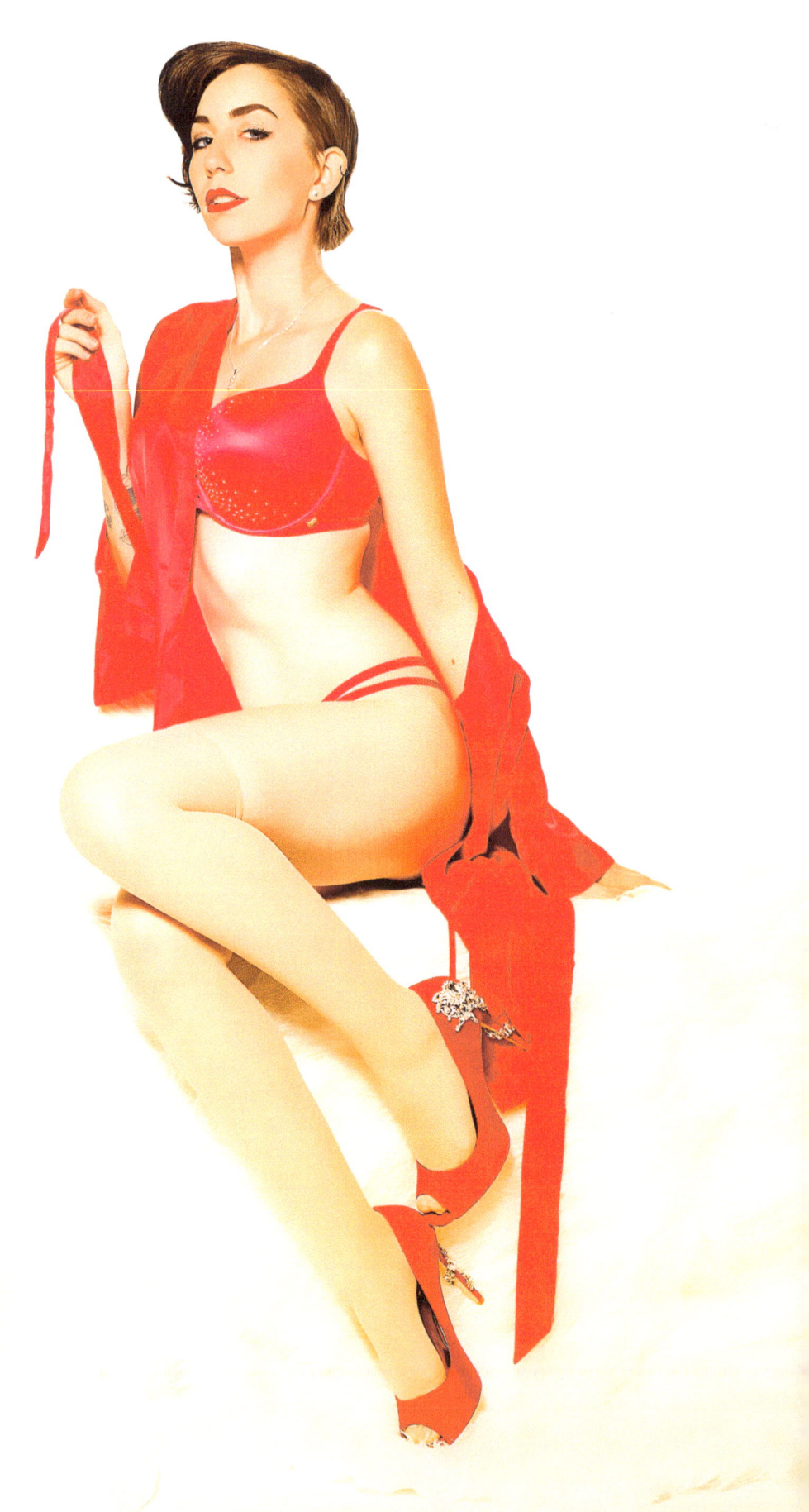

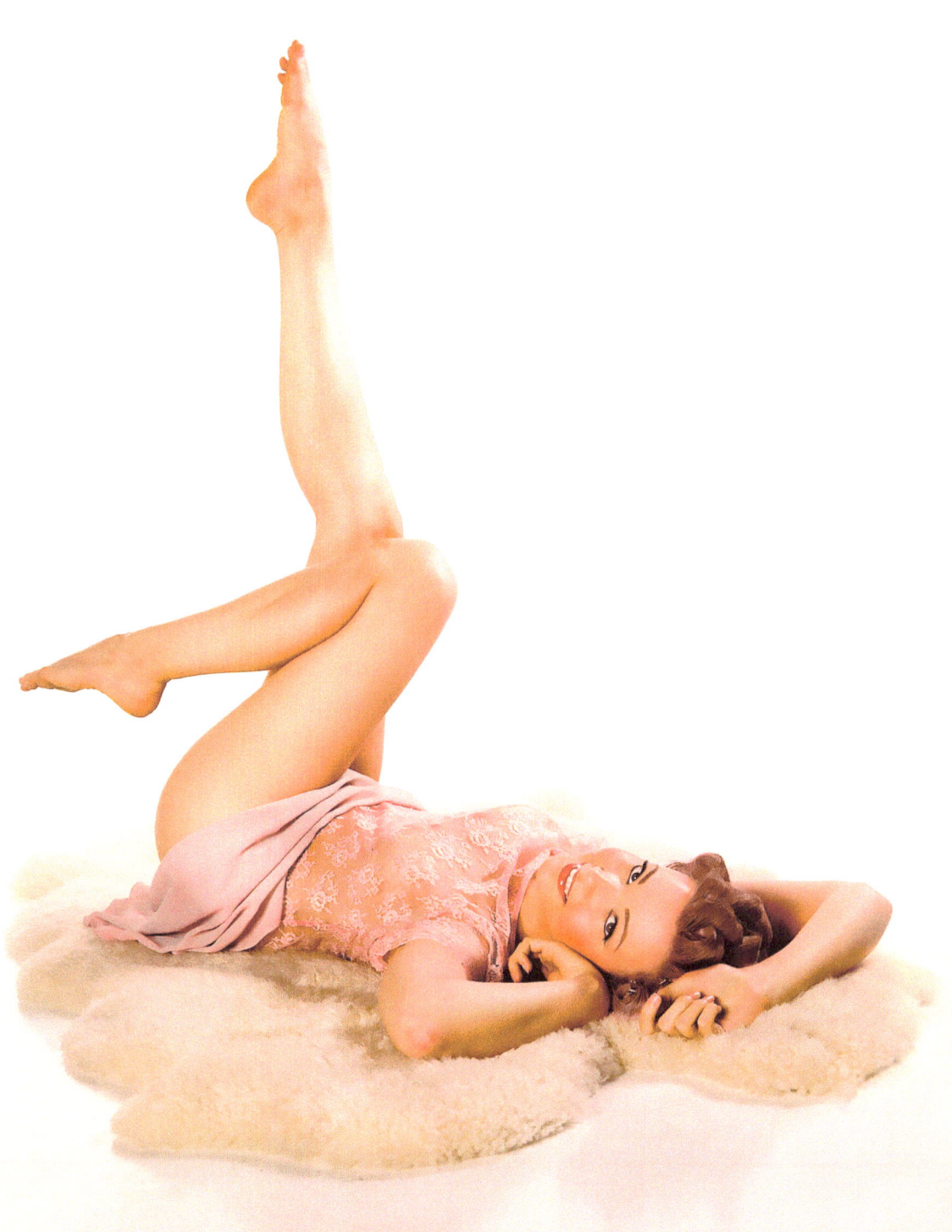

HOLIDAY THEME PINUPS

HALLOWEEN, VALENTINE'S DAY, ST. PATRICK'S DAY, 4TH OF JULY, CHRISTMAS.

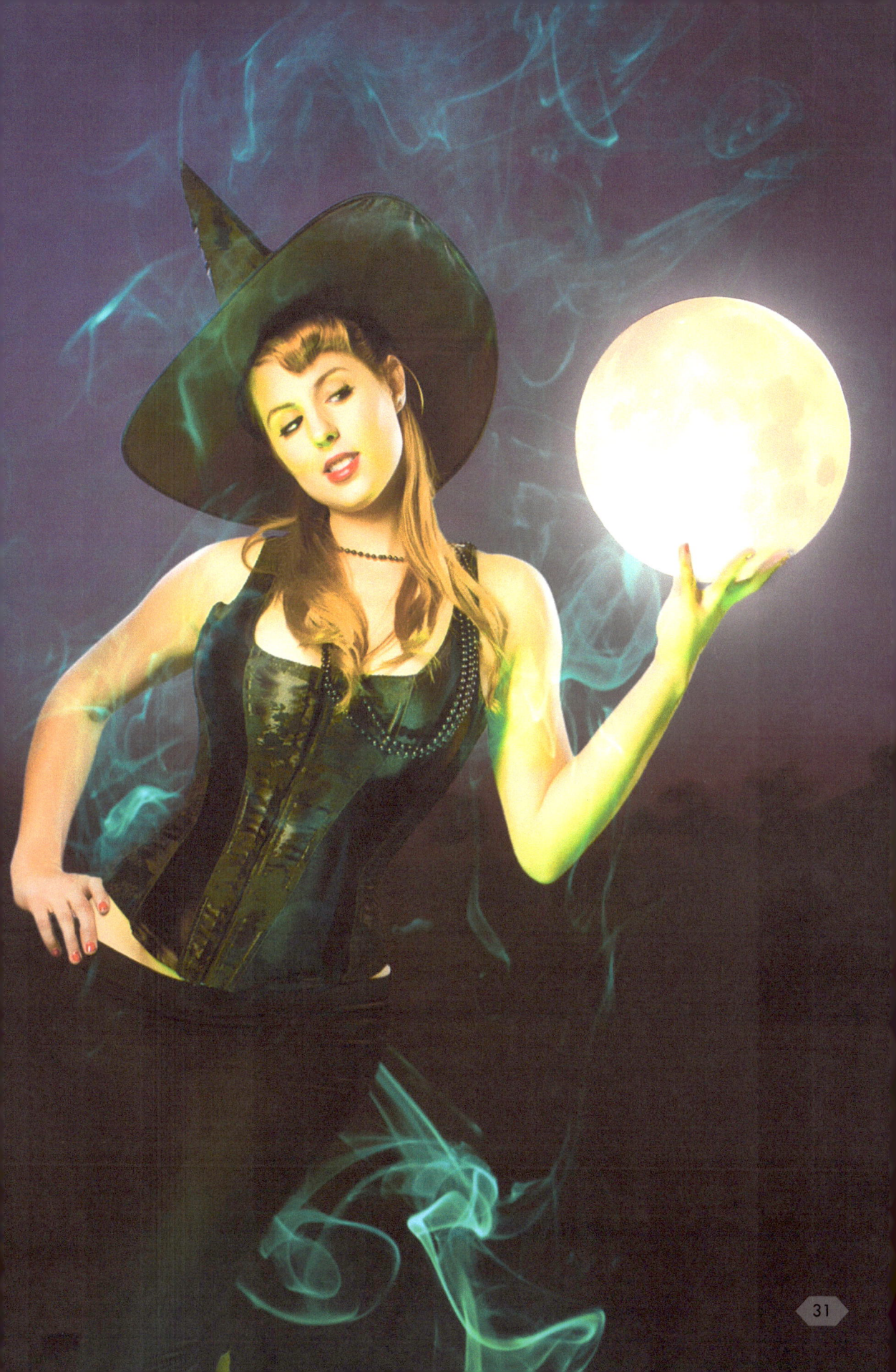

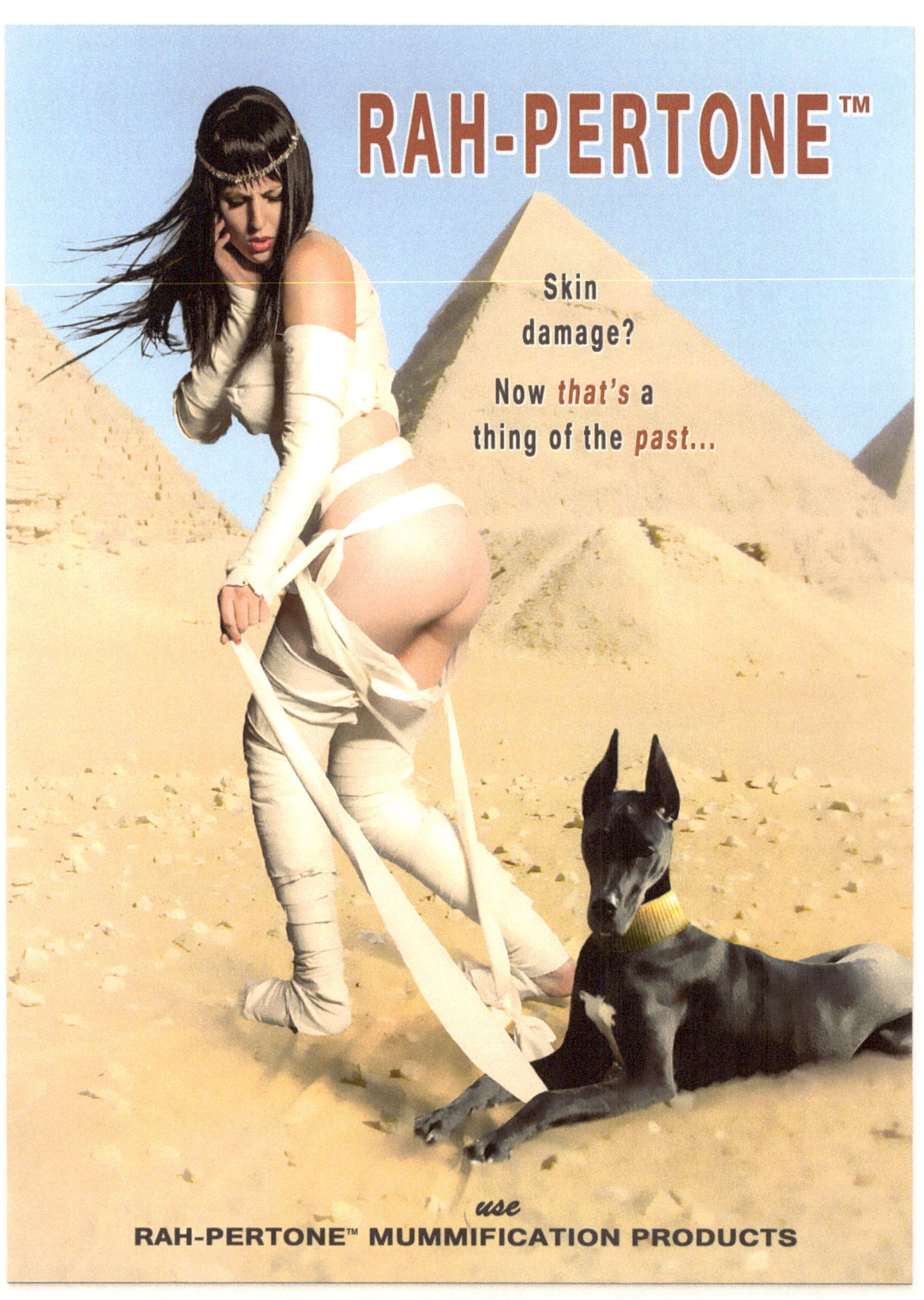

Eternity may seem like forever but try to...

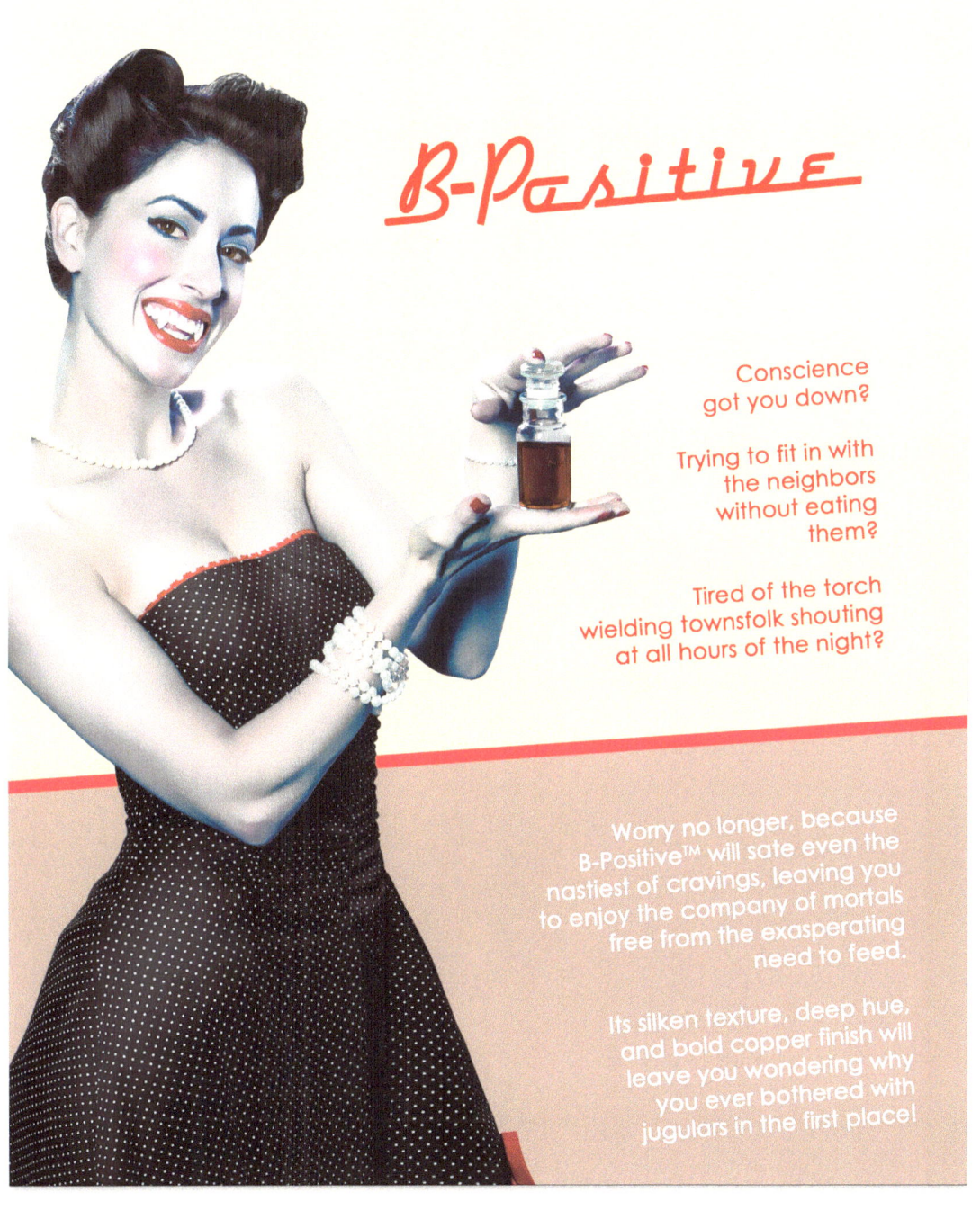

B-Positive

Conscience got you down?

Trying to fit in with the neighbors without eating them?

Tired of the torch wielding townsfolk shouting at all hours of the night?

Worry no longer, because B-Positive™ will sate even the nastiest of cravings, leaving you to enjoy the company of mortals free from the exasperating need to feed.

Its silken texture, deep hue, and bold copper finish will leave you wondering why you ever bothered with jugulars in the first place!

BEHIND THE SCENES

INSPIRATION
The pose and subject were inspired by the classic Marilyn Monroe floating skirt photograph.

EDITING
Because of the active nature of the pose, the top and bottom half of the model were two different photos.

INSIDER INFO
Capturing the right skirt flip effect was a challenge during this shoot. This take was achieved with help from a friend who would toss the skirt and then leap off-set. You can barely see the elbow of the friend's arm on the edge of the original photo.

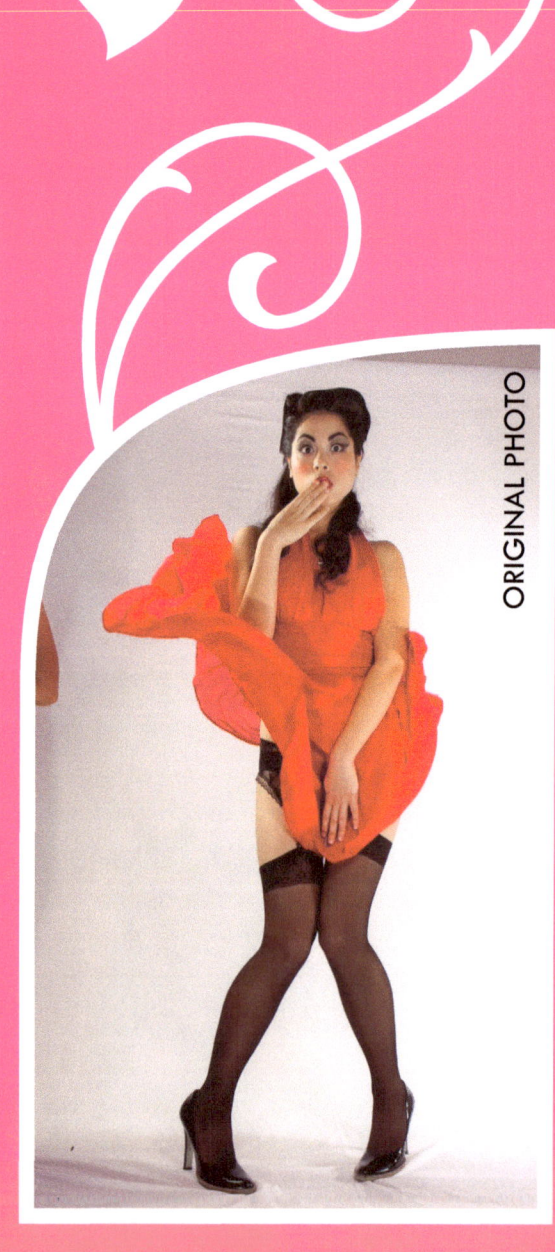

ORIGINAL PHOTO

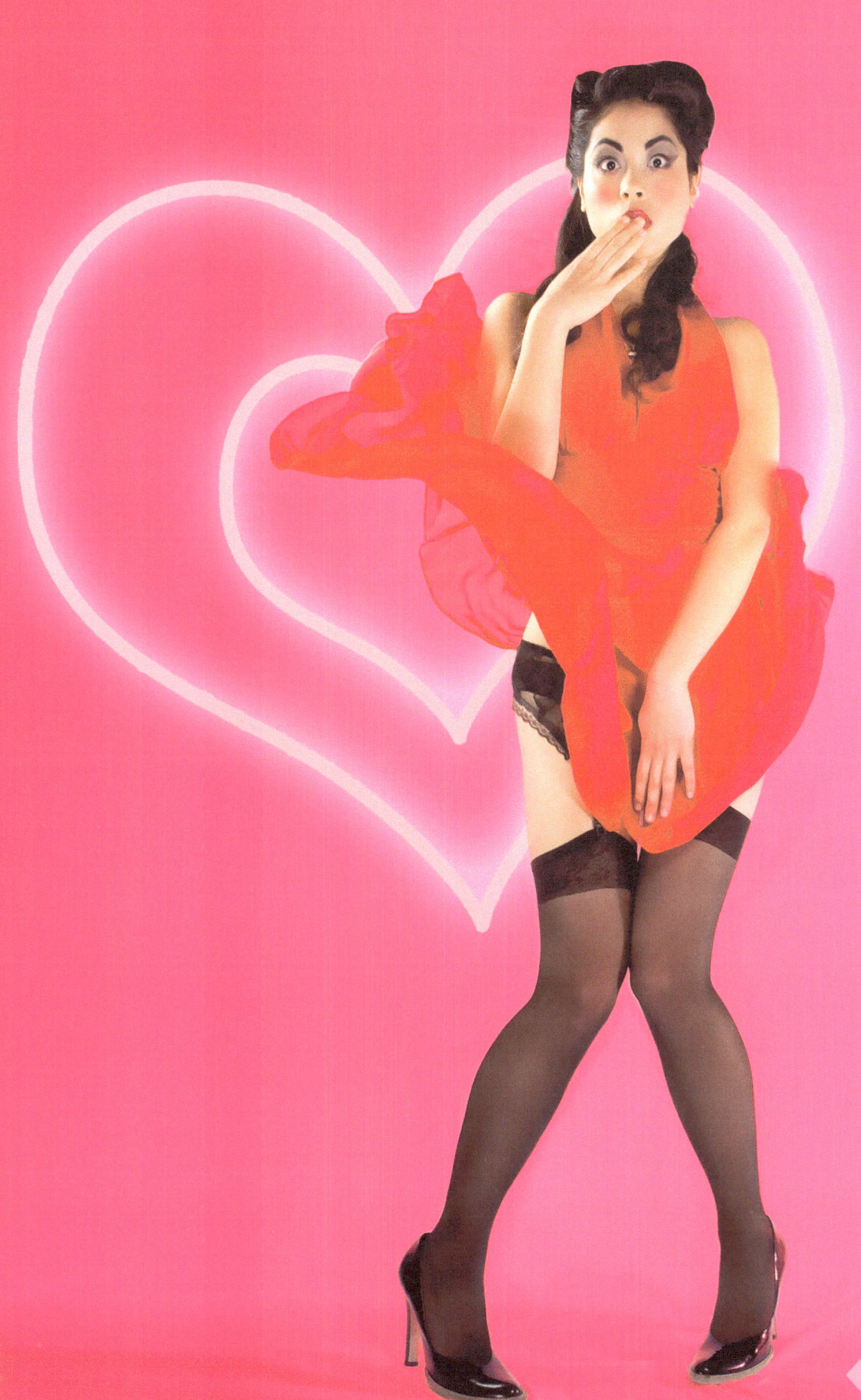

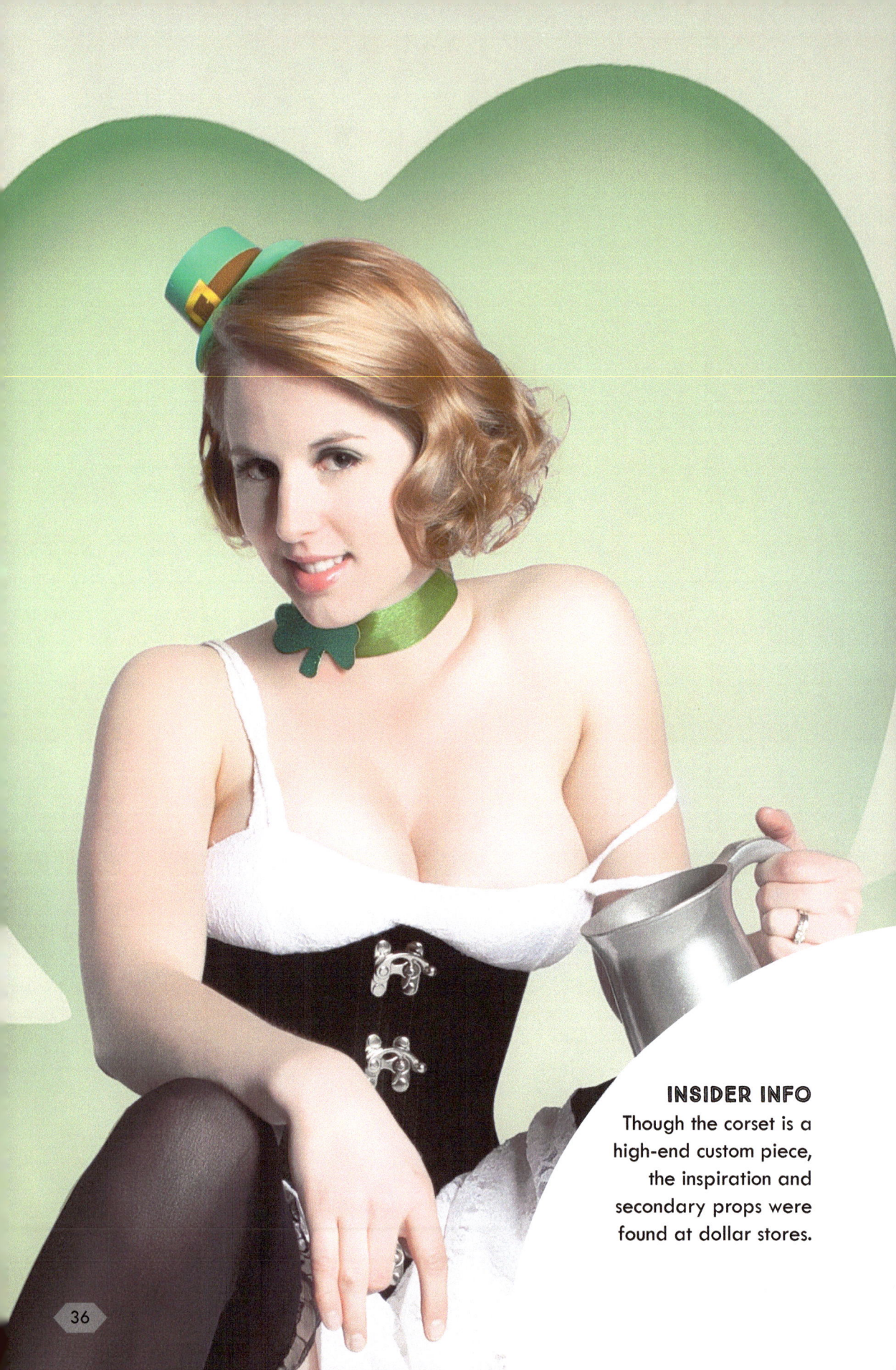

INSIDER INFO
Though the corset is a
high-end custom piece,
the inspiration and
secondary props were
found at dollar stores.

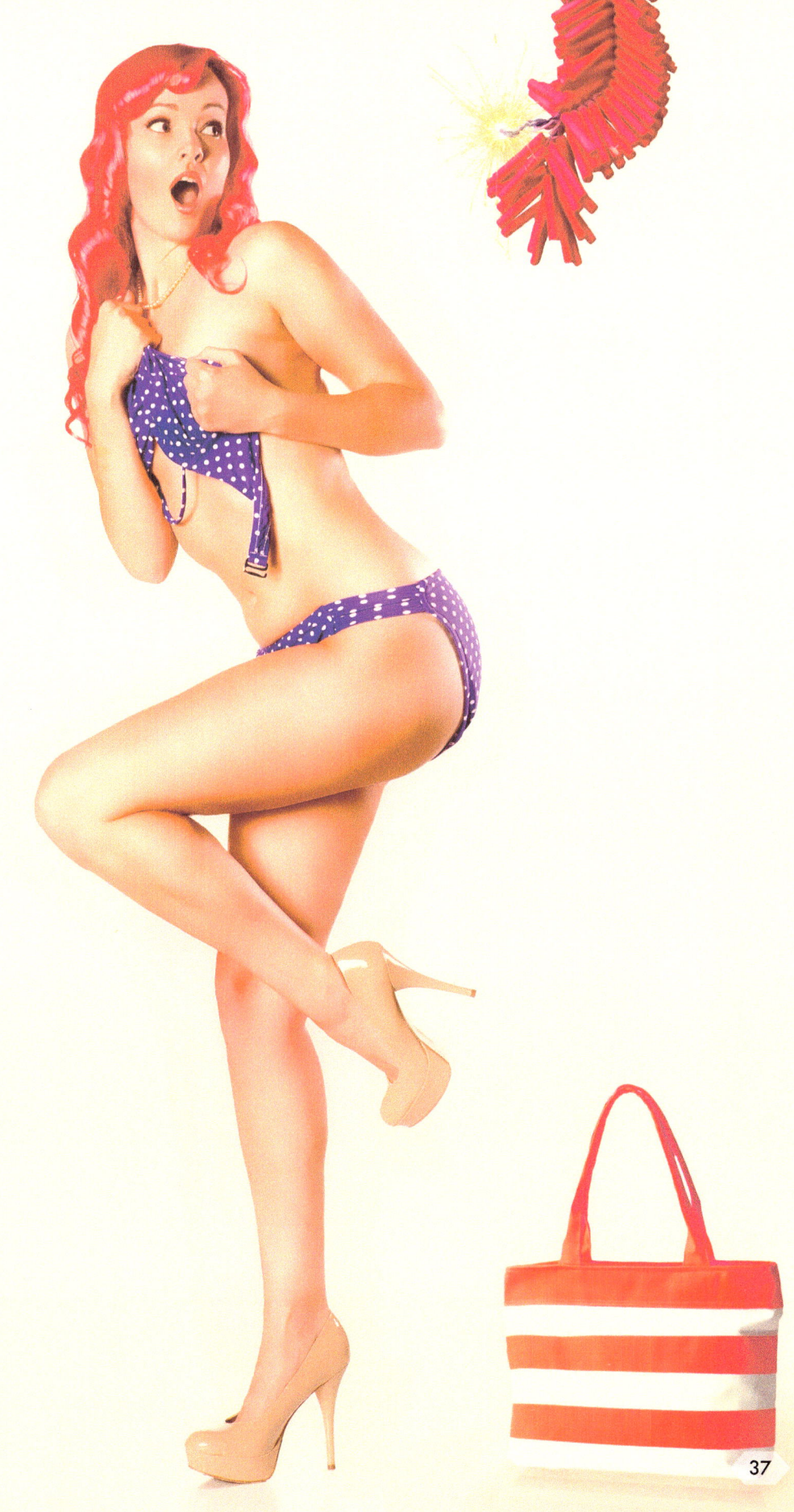

Don't be fooled - this pose is a LOT harder than it looks - the model is basically folded in half in the box.

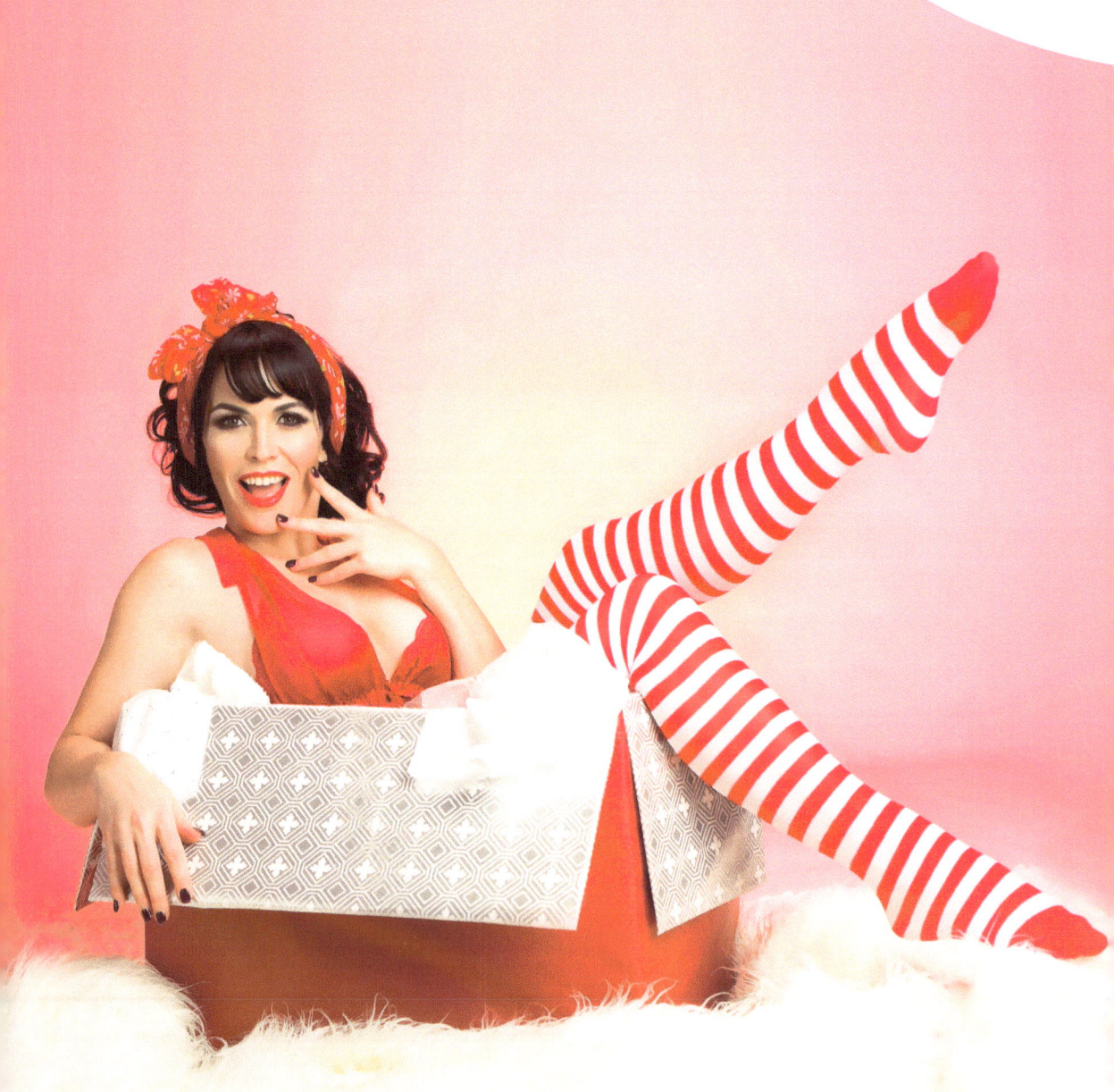

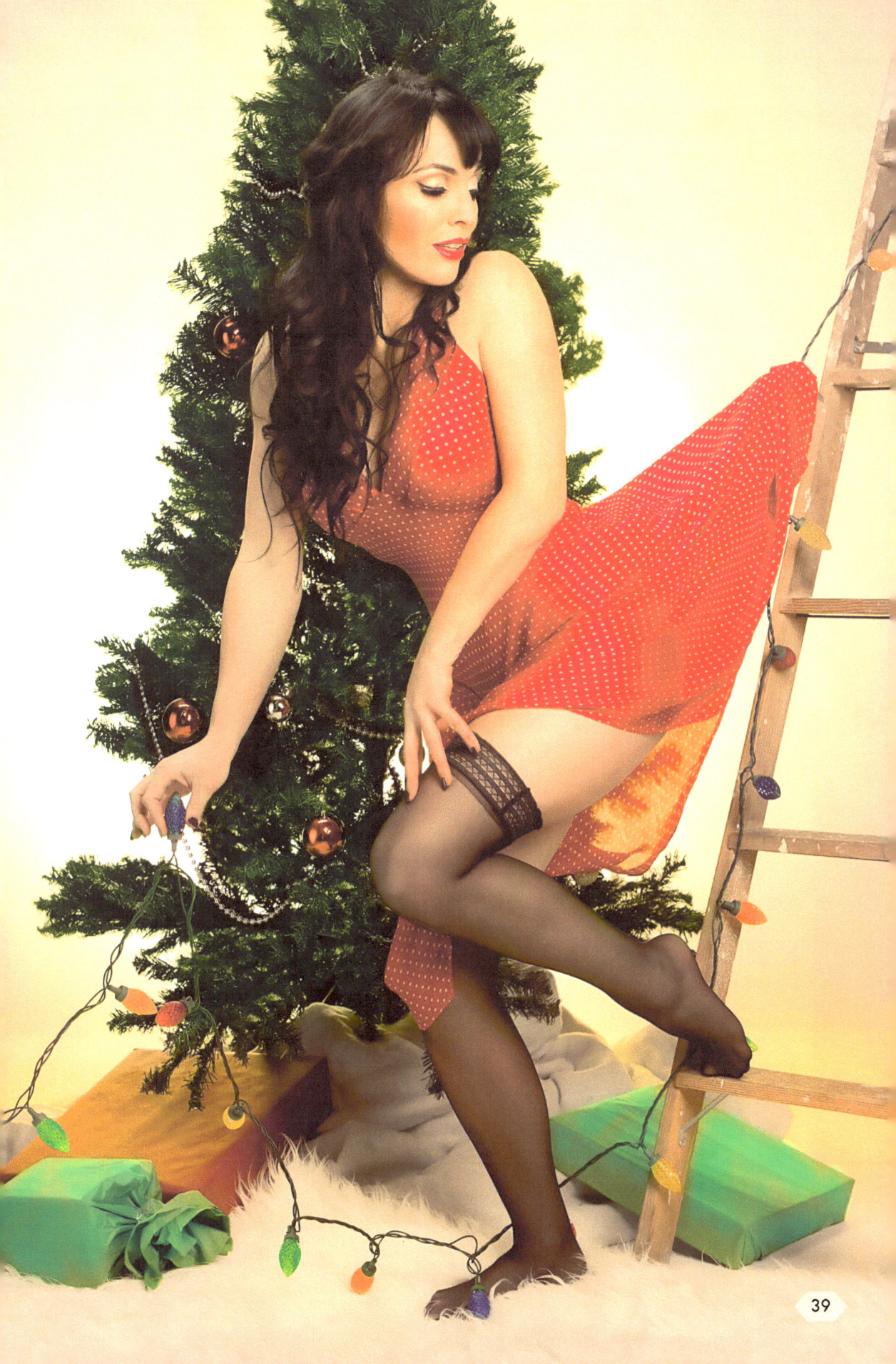

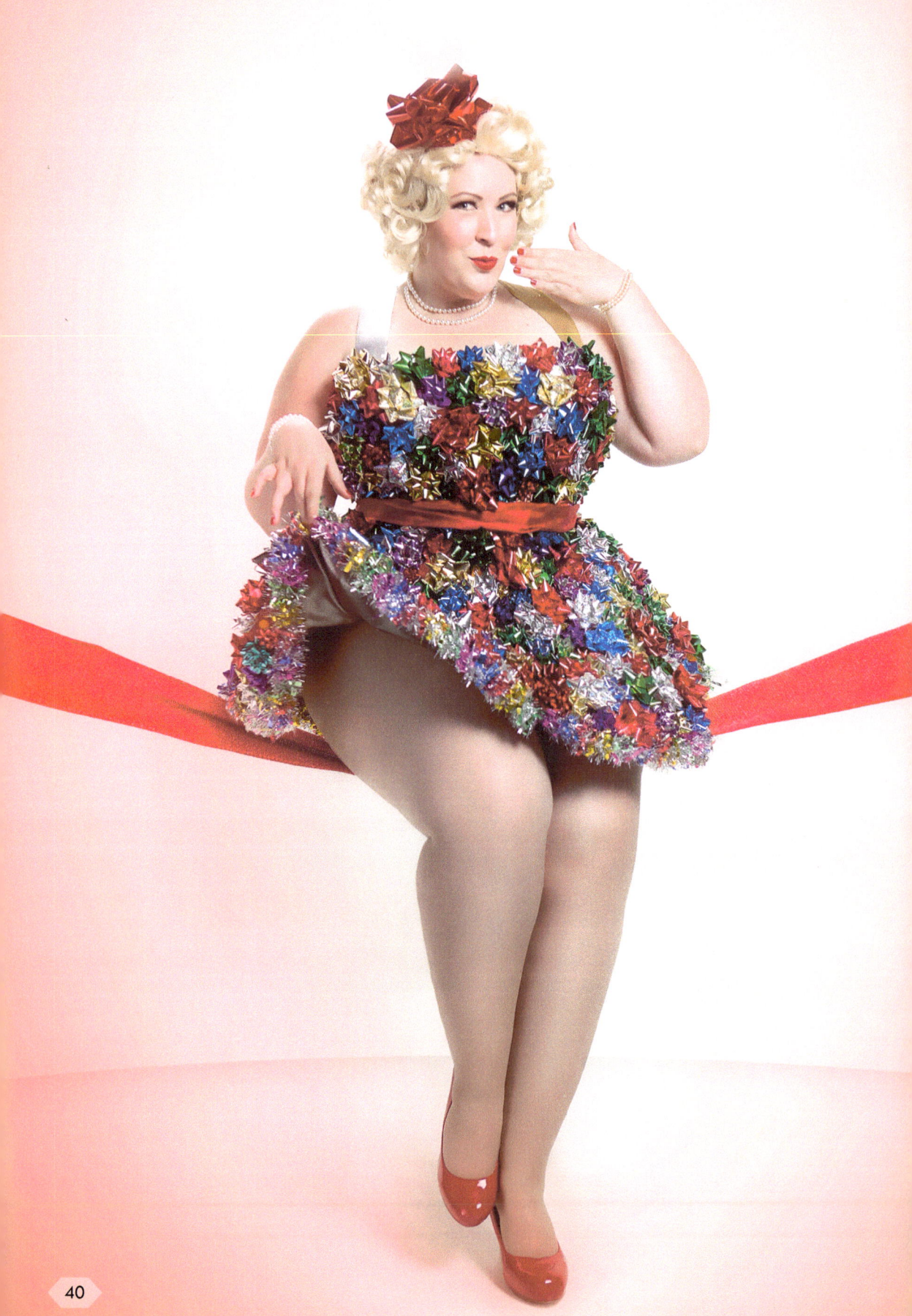

BEHIND THE SCENES

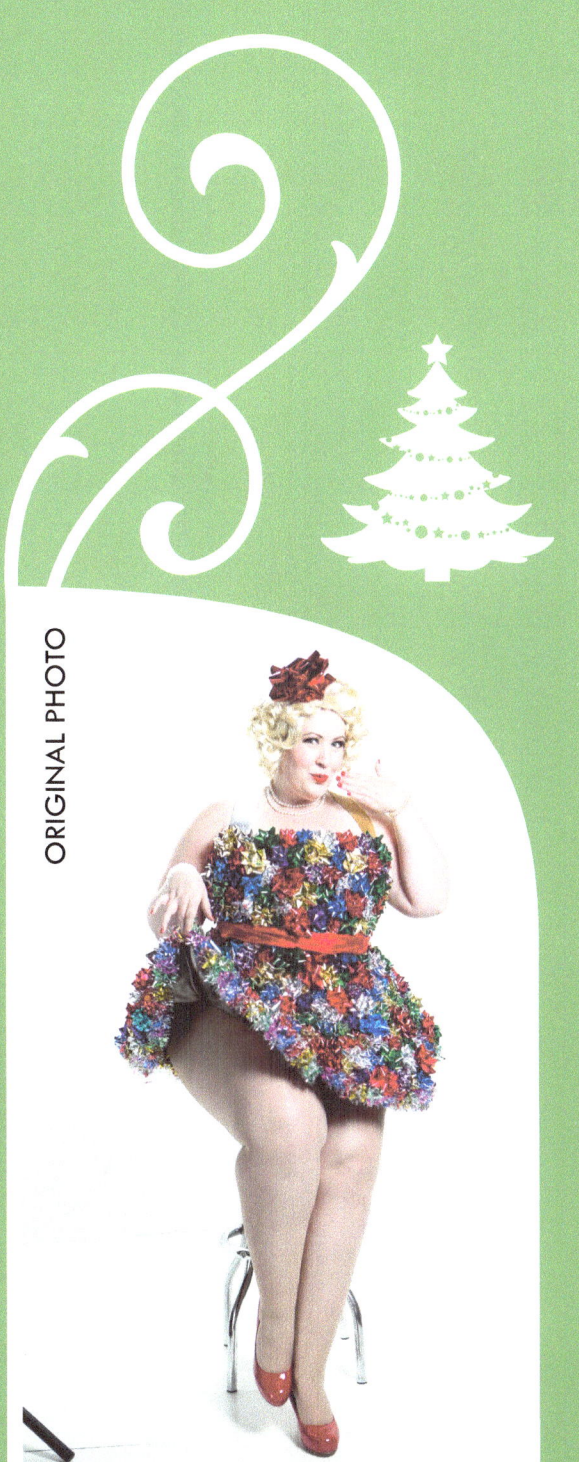

ORIGINAL PHOTO

INSPIRATION
This Christmas-themed shoot was inspired by the playful idea of wrapping oneself up in gift wrap - a present both naughty and nice!

EDITING
First the stool was digitally removed and then replaced with a picture of a twisted ribbon that was photographed later.

INSIDER INFO
The model acquired this hand-made ultra-creative bow dress to use in this shoot. Woven into the dress were actual Christmas lights, so the dress could light up and blink using a battery pack!

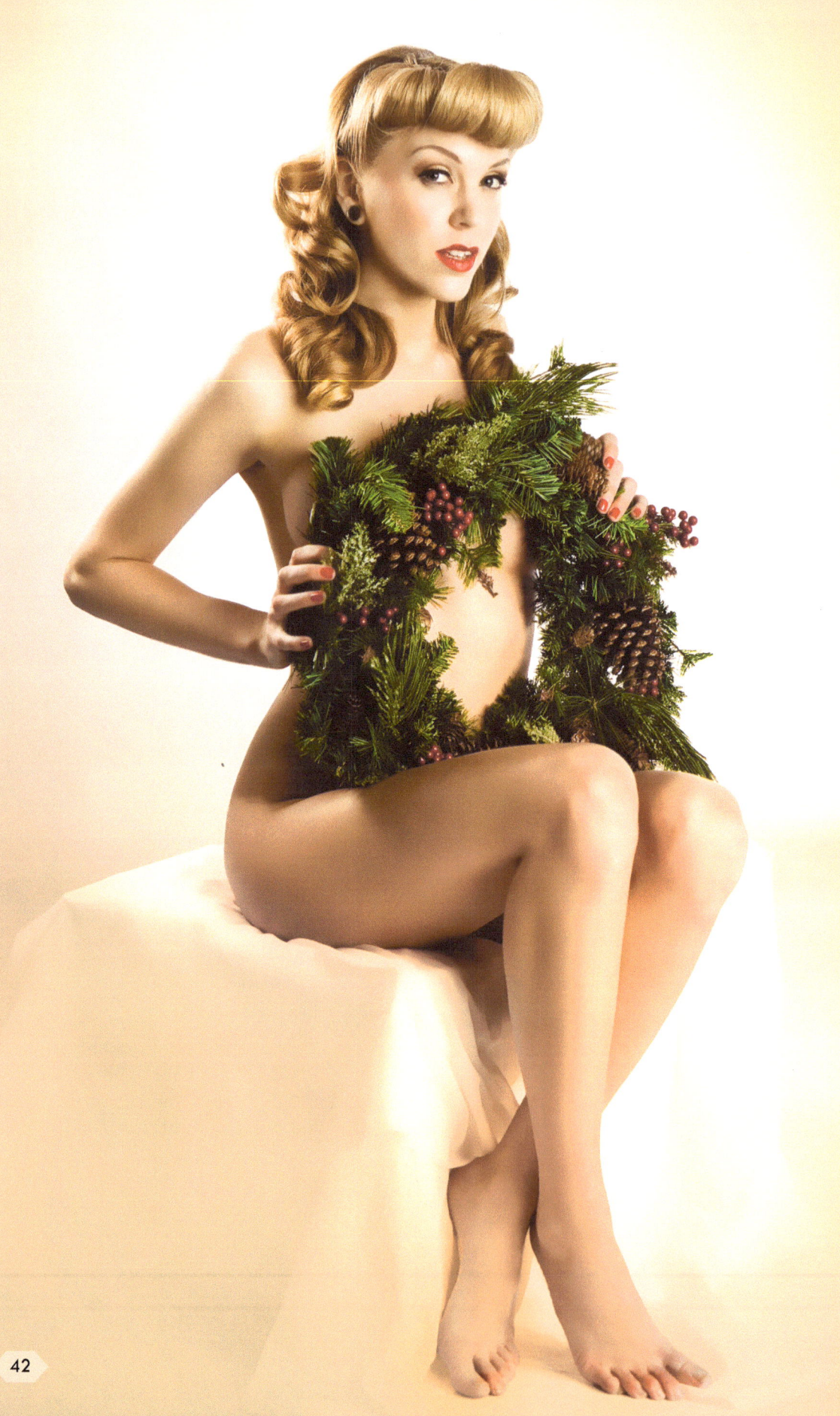

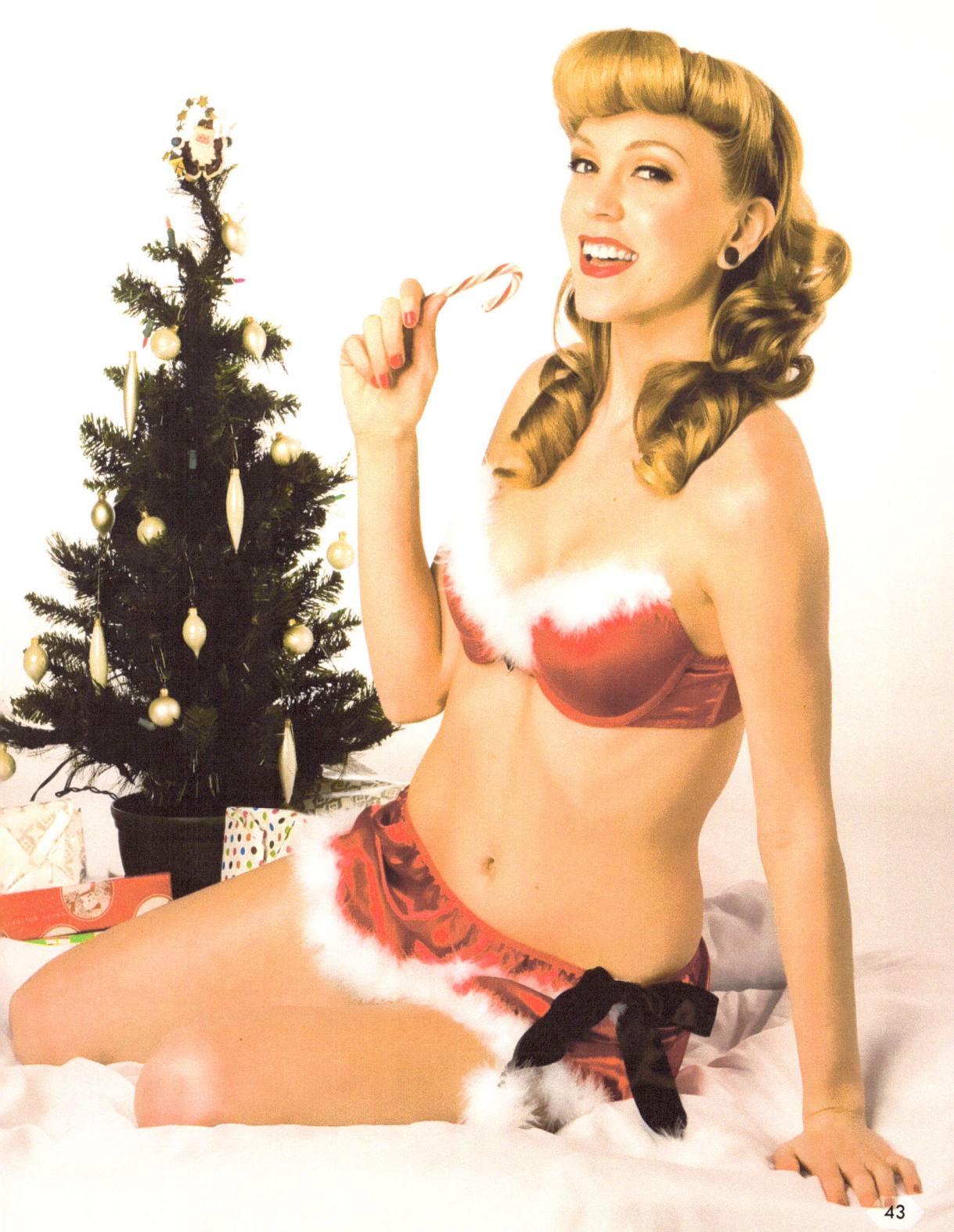

MILITARY & PATRIOTIC PINUPS

ARMY, SAILOR, FIREFIGHTER, FLAG, AIR FORCE, RUSSIAN TANK, SUBMARINE, GUN, AND BOMB.

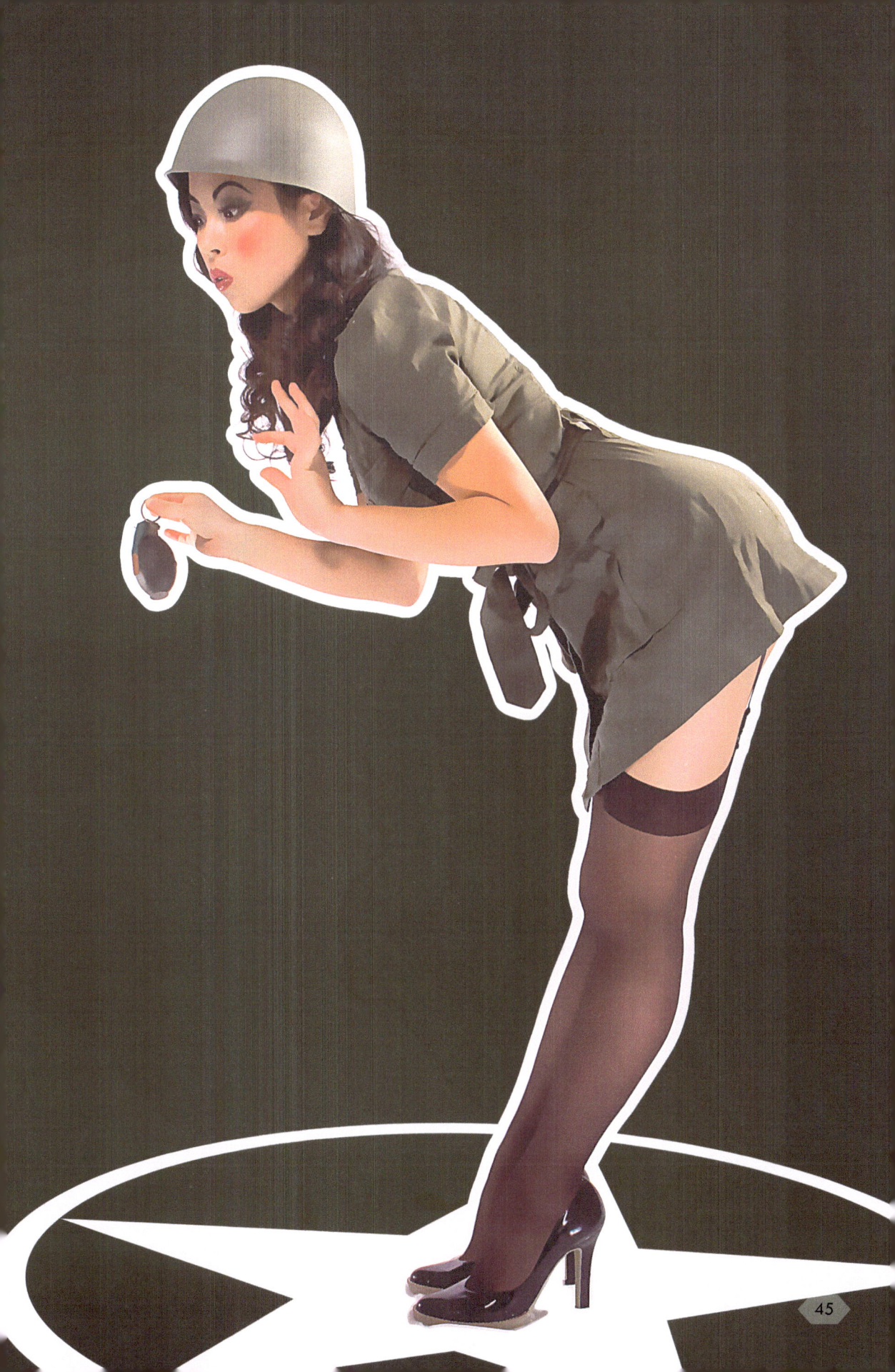

BEHIND THE SCENES

INSPIRATION
The naughty sailor theme is practically a tradition in pinup.

EDITING
First the extraneous elements were removed and background and mast pole replaced. Next, a 'painter' style adjustment effect is added to the model's dress and skin to give it a more surreal feel.

INSIDER INFO
A handy shop-clip works wonders to hold the dress back as if it were being blown in the wind. A cardboard tube substitutes for the ship mast pole.

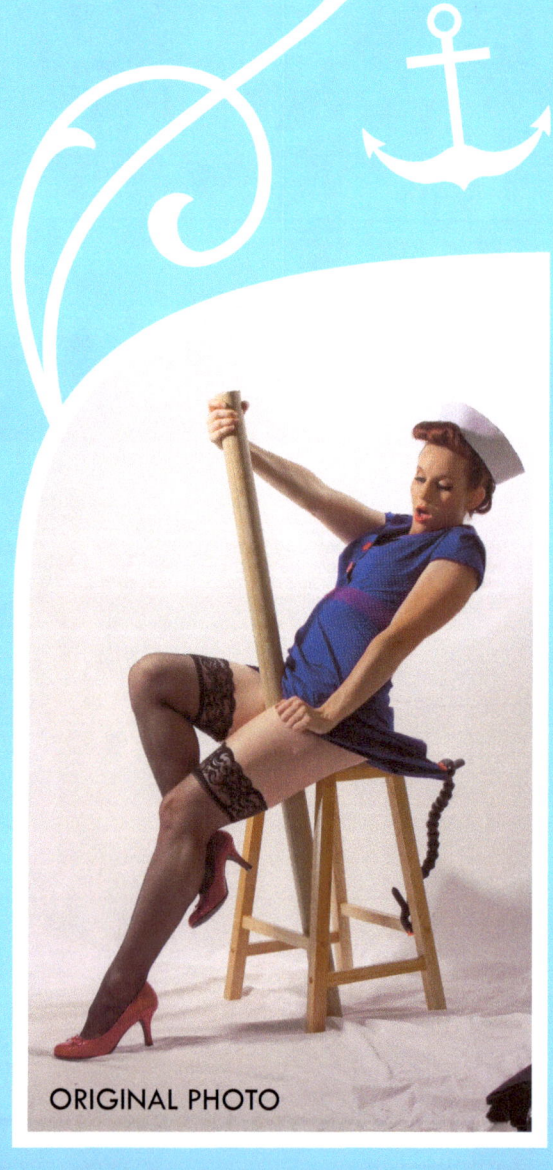
ORIGINAL PHOTO

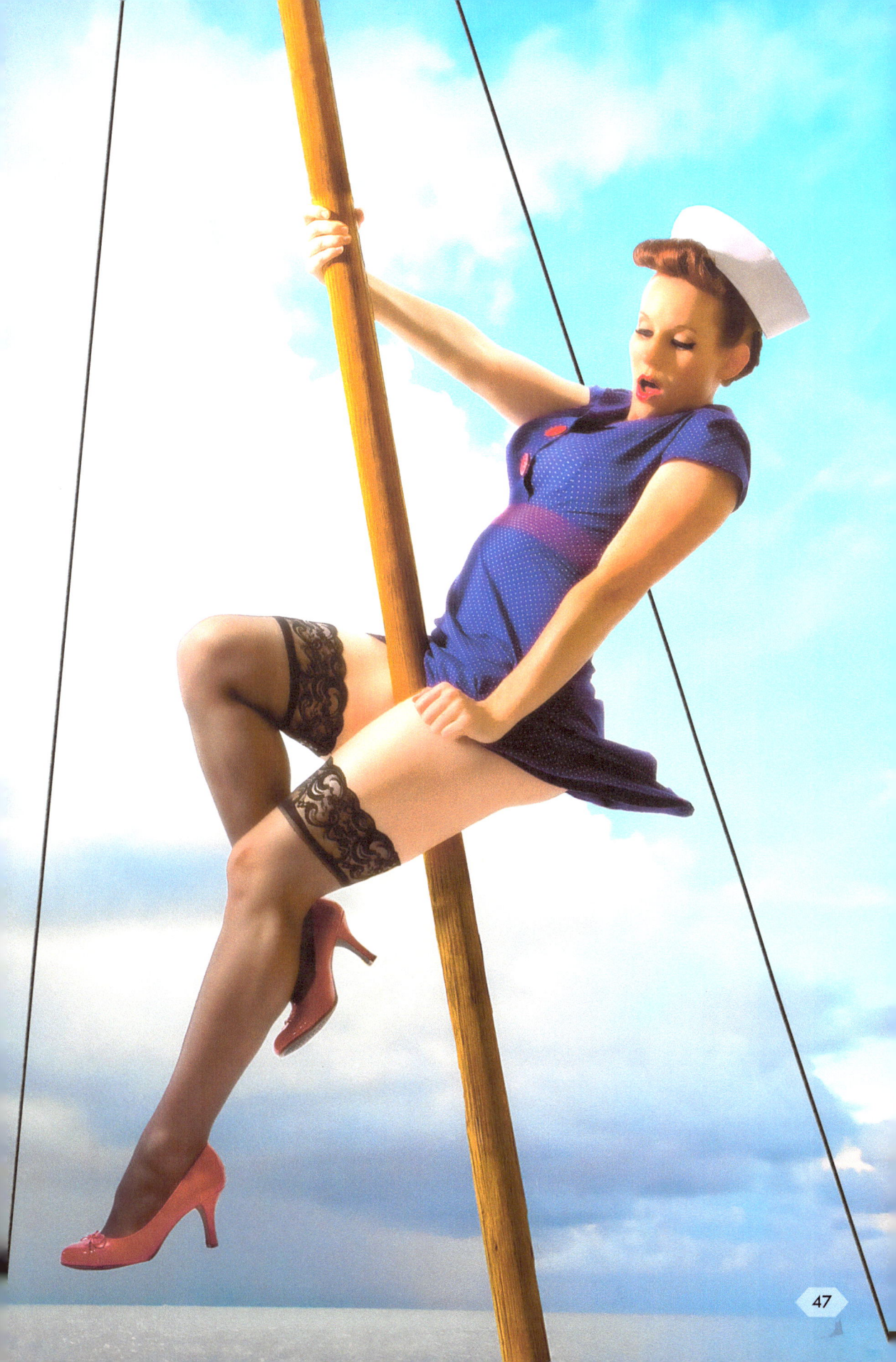

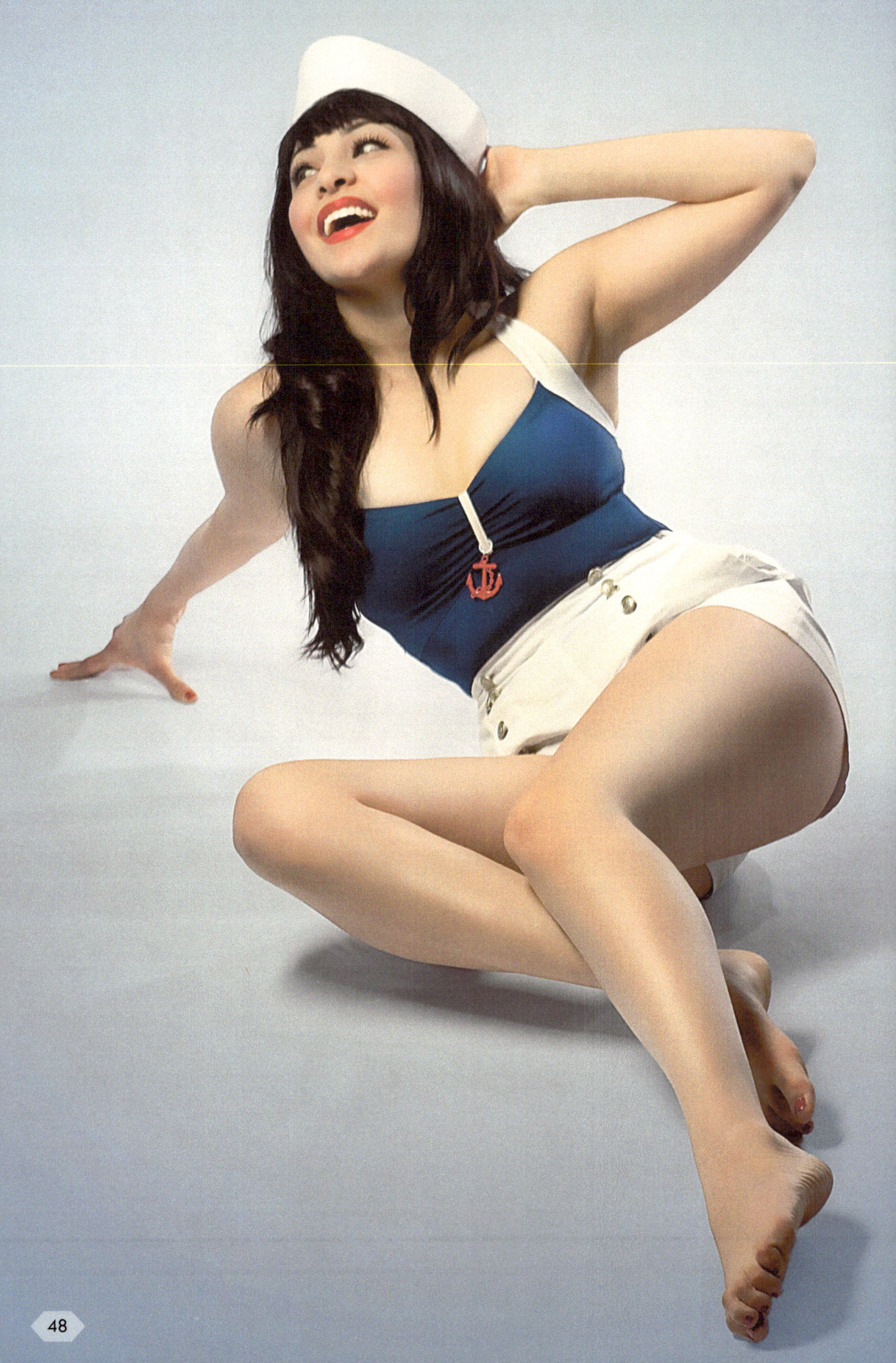

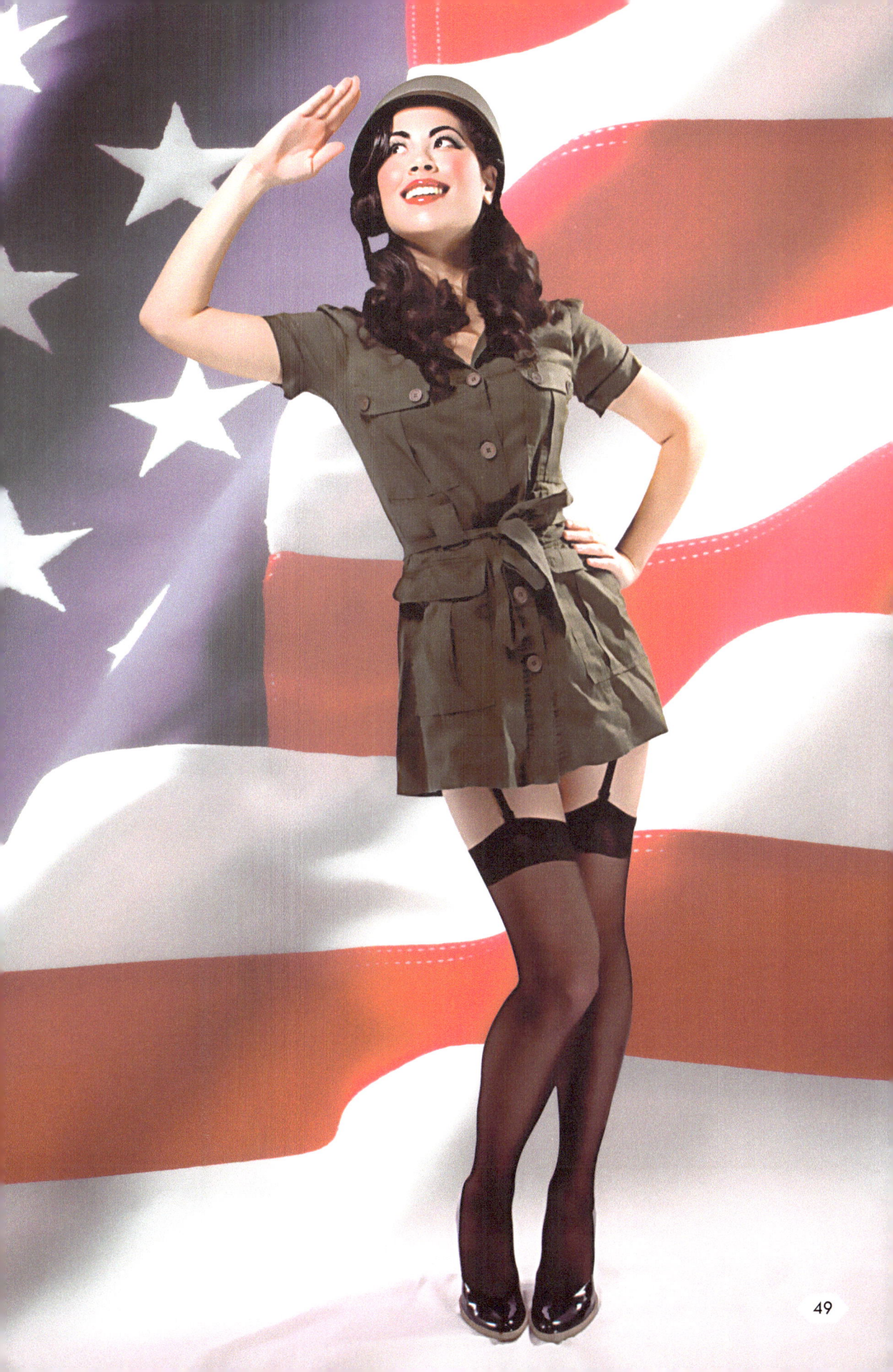

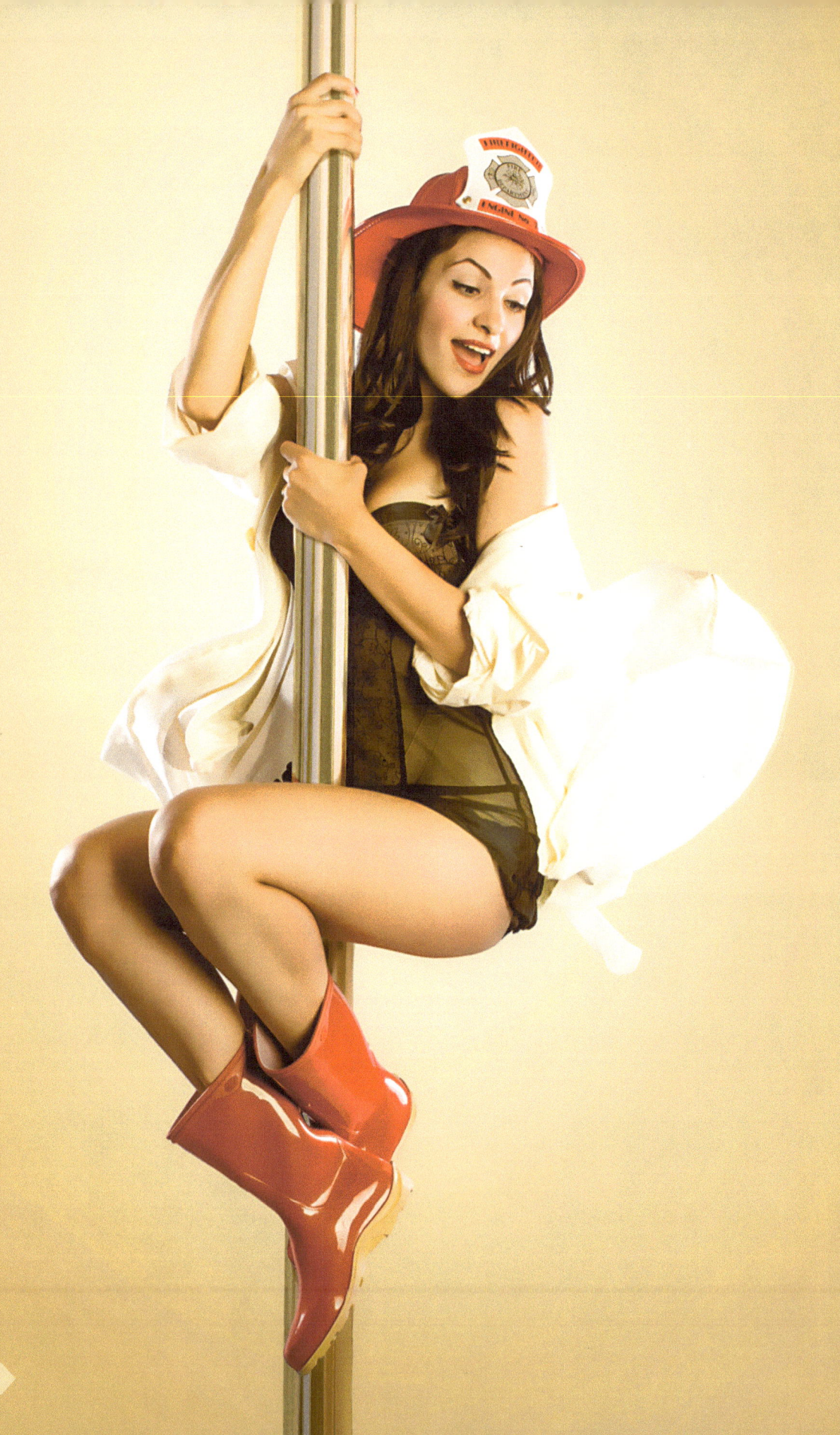

BEHIND THE SCENES

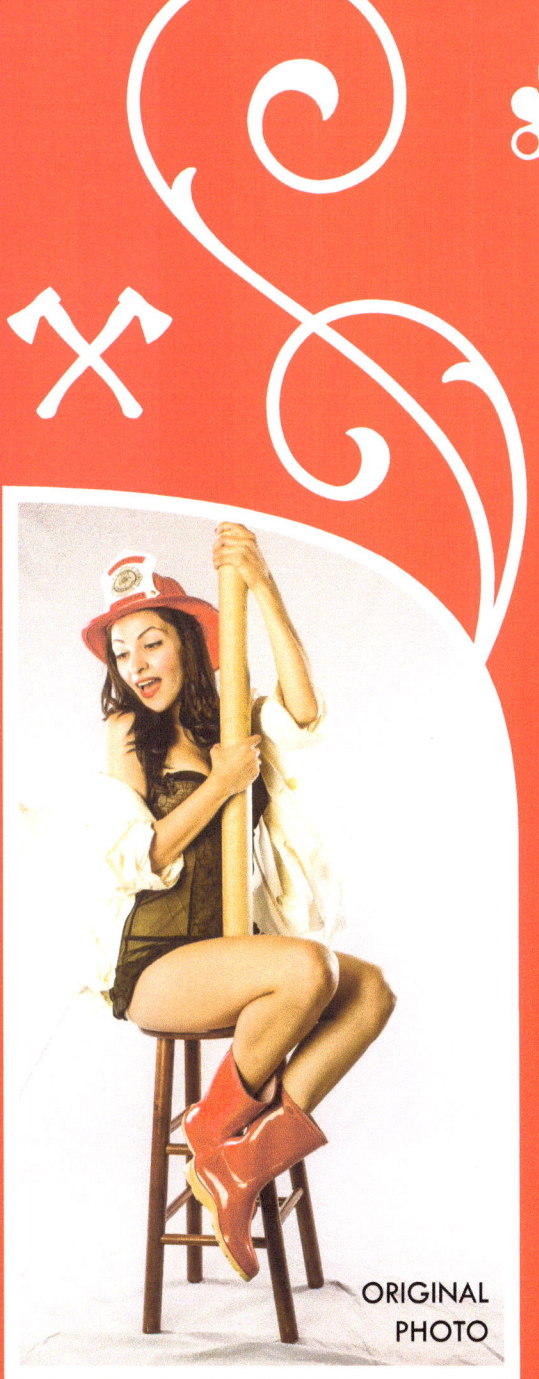

ORIGINAL PHOTO

INSPIRATION
An homage to the famous firefighter pinup girl by Gil Elvgren.

EDITING
After the stool and background were removed, the firefighter pole was recreated in 3D with the original image applied as a reflection.

INSIDER INFO
The model's sister was on set during this shoot and the photographer recruited her help with flinging the white jacket into the air and leaping off-set as the photo was taken. A cardboard tube substitutes perfectly for the fire pole.

BEHIND THE SCENES

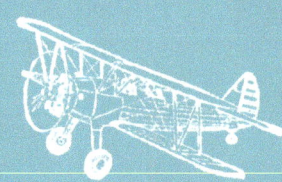

INSPIRATION
Recreating the weathered photo that a pilot might keep of their sweetheart in the cockpit was the vision for this shoot.

LOCATION
This photo shoot took place at an aviation museum in northern California - the museum allowed the model special permission to touch and climb inside the display planes!

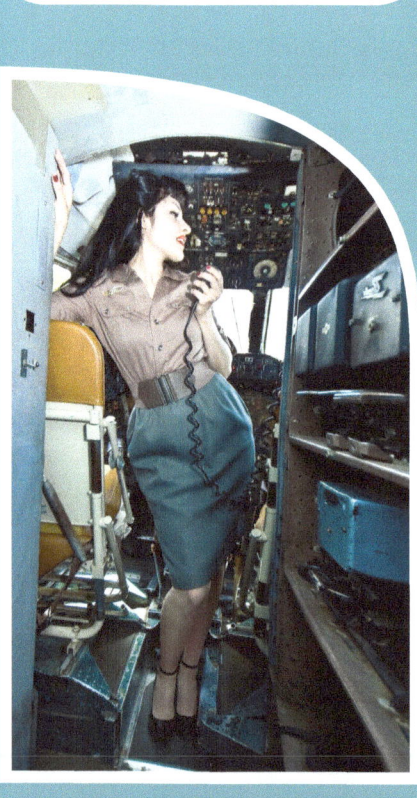

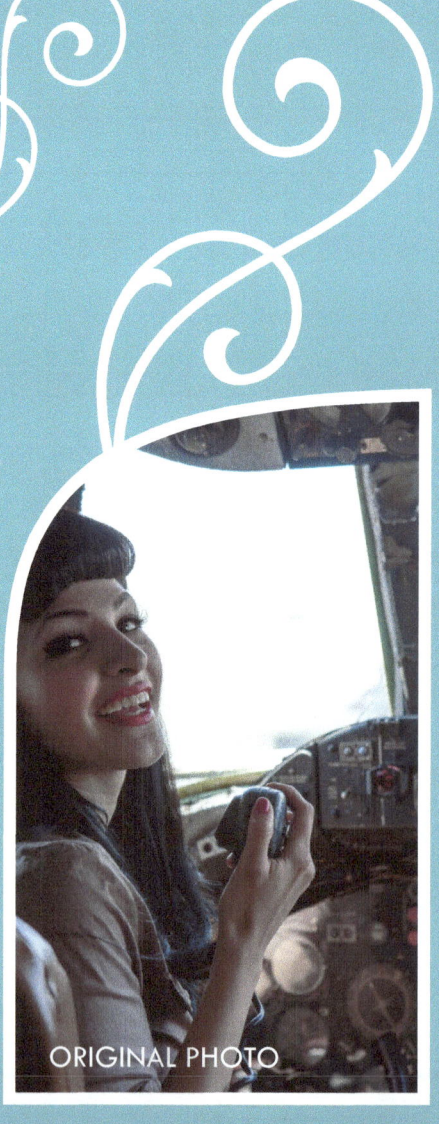

ORIGINAL PHOTO

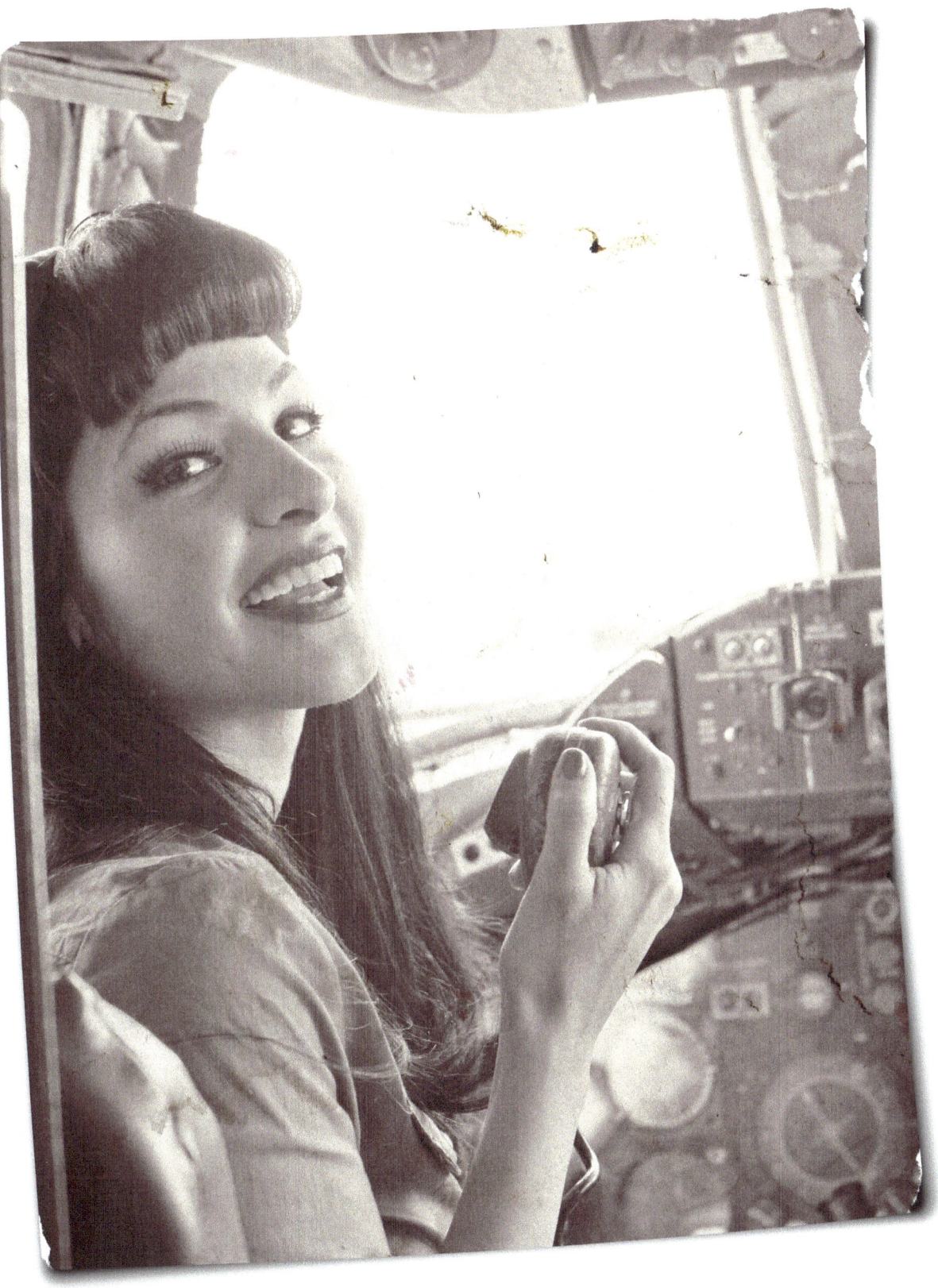

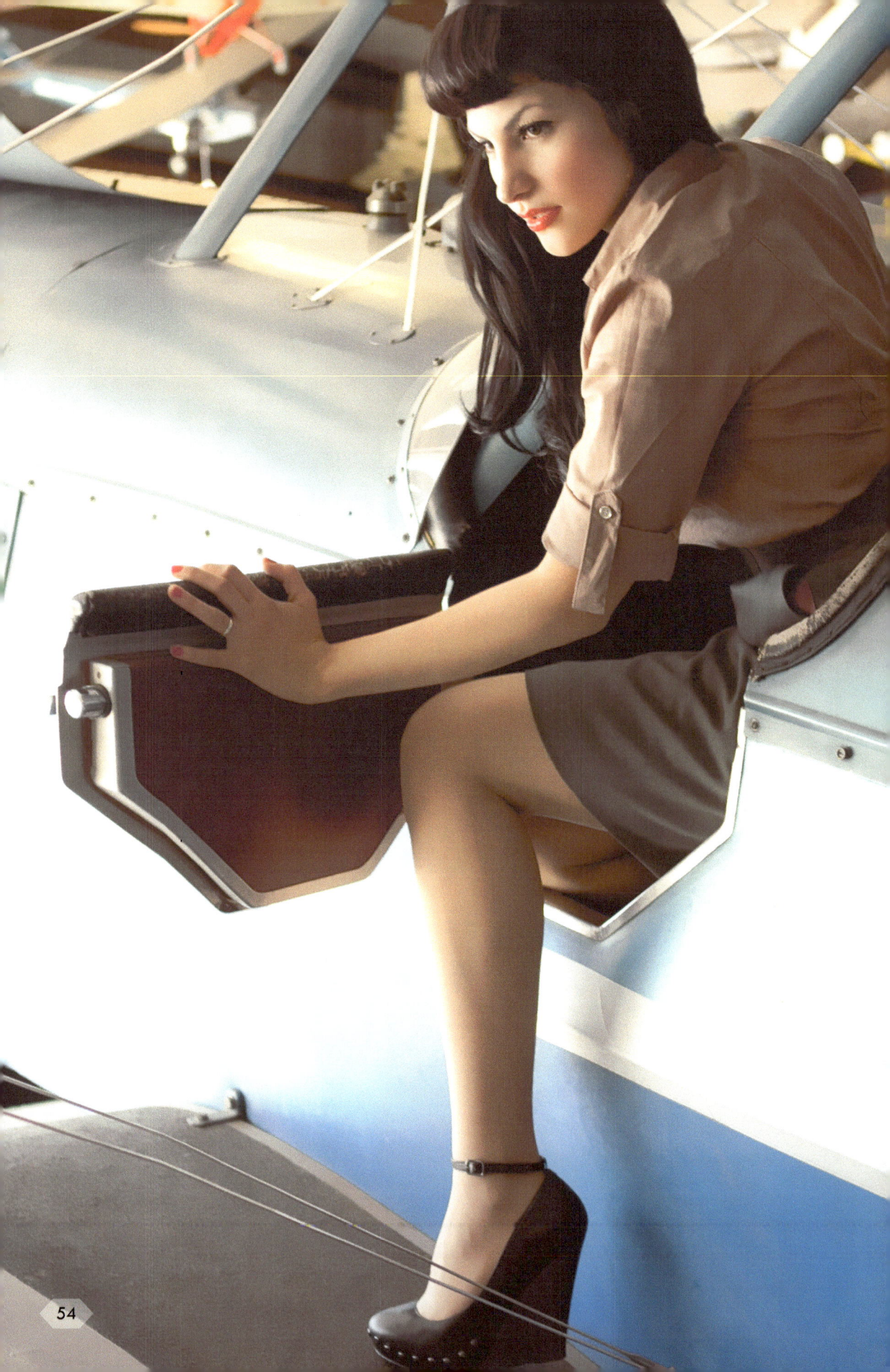

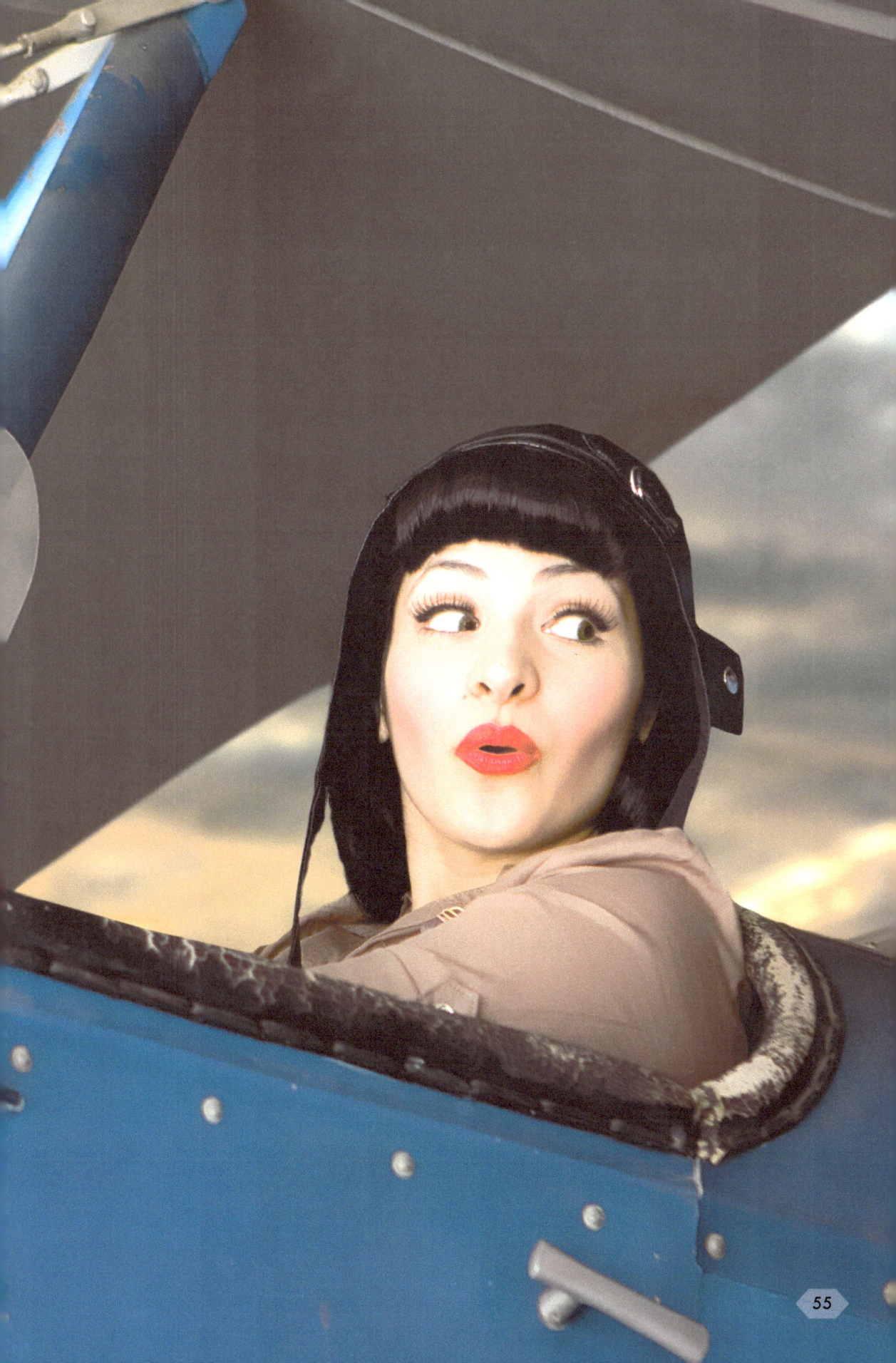

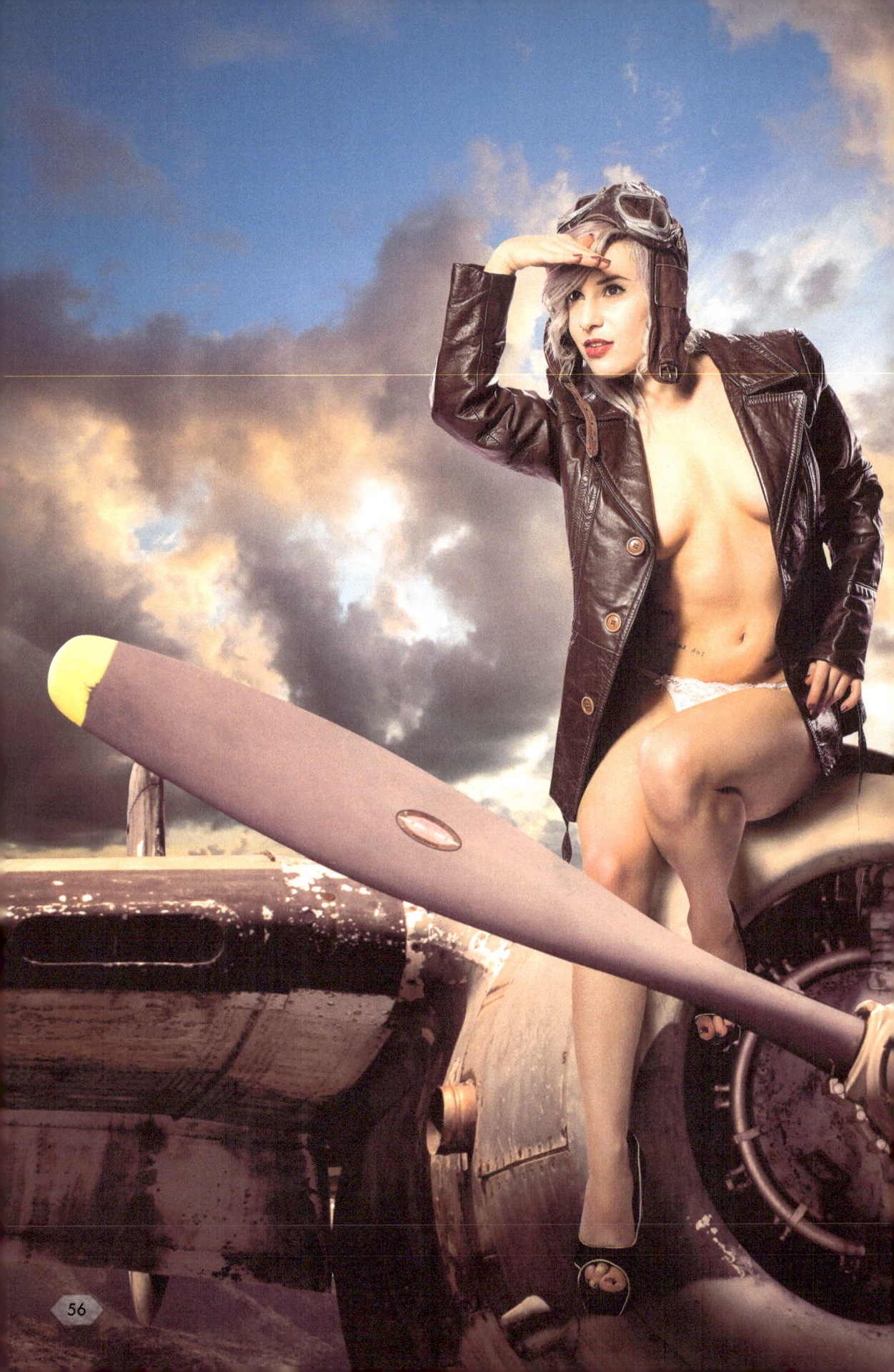

BEHIND THE SCENES

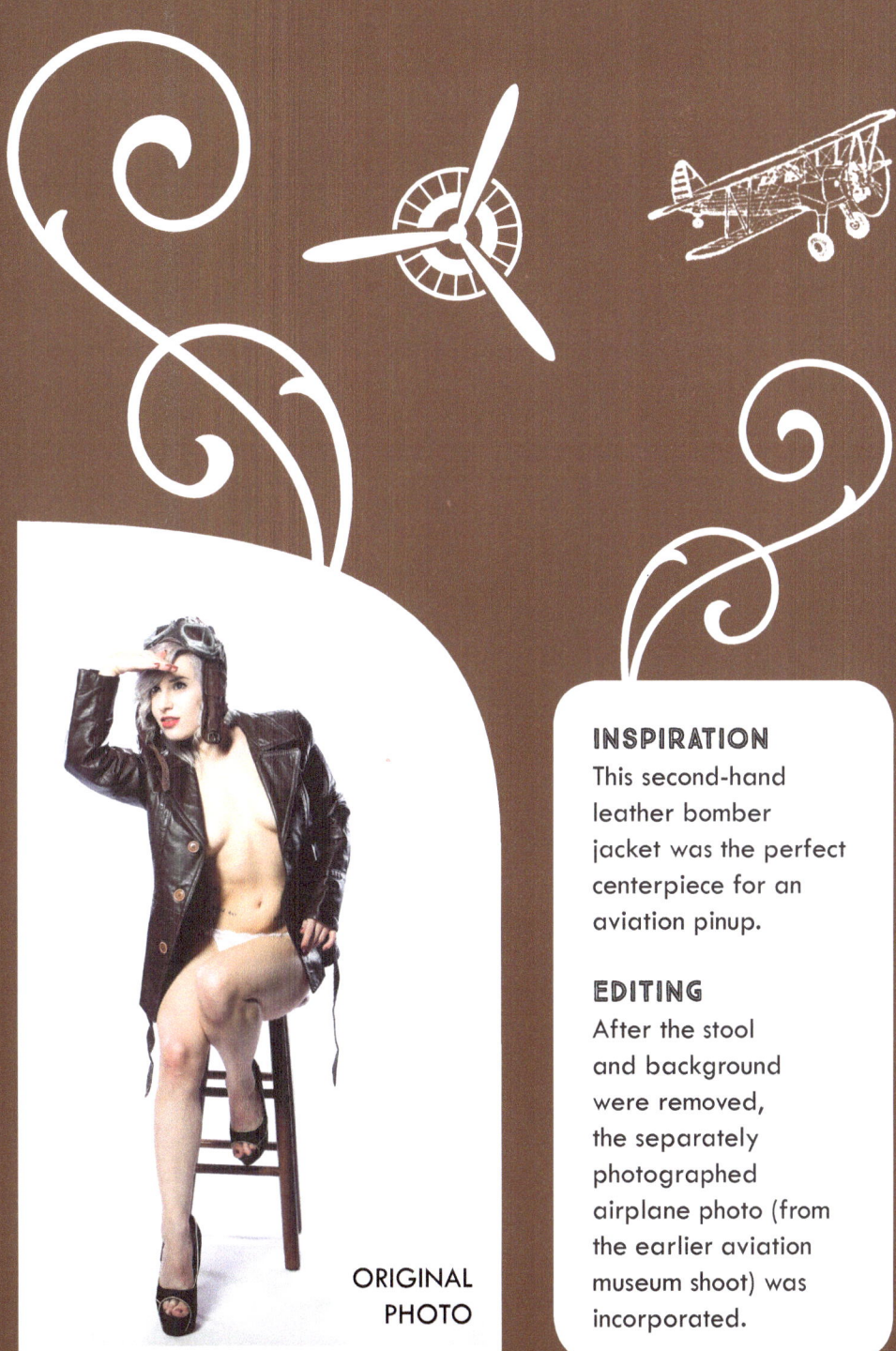

ORIGINAL
PHOTO

INSPIRATION
This second-hand
leather bomber
jacket was the perfect
centerpiece for an
aviation pinup.

EDITING
After the stool
and background
were removed,
the separately
photographed
airplane photo (from
the earlier aviation
museum shoot) was
incorporated.

BEHIND THE SCENES

INSPIRATION
Finding this old hat at a thrift shop was the entire inspiration behind this series of Russian military themed shots.

EDITING
Swapping in an entirely new background can be challenging. This military bomb imagery was officially released by the government into the public domain. It is one of the atom bomb tests performed during WWII.

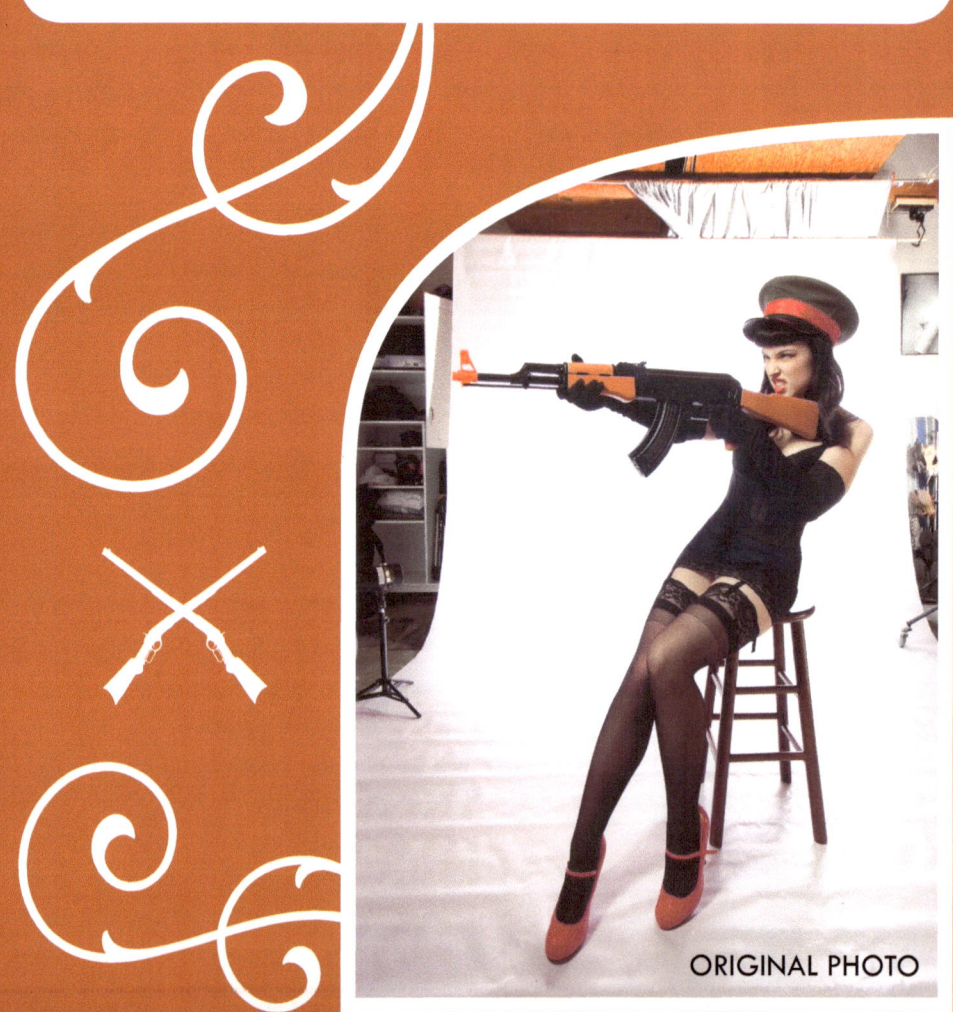

ORIGINAL PHOTO

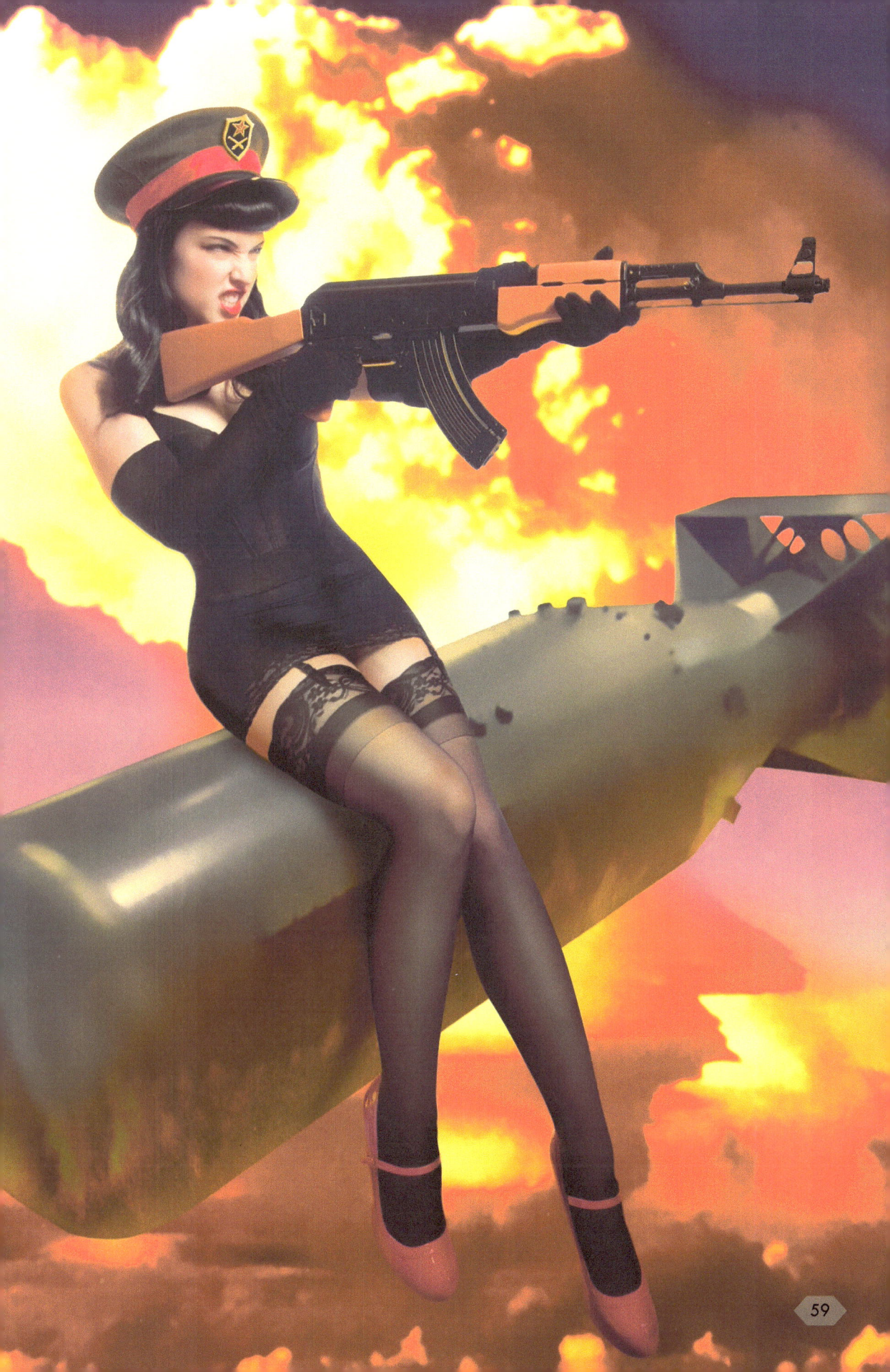

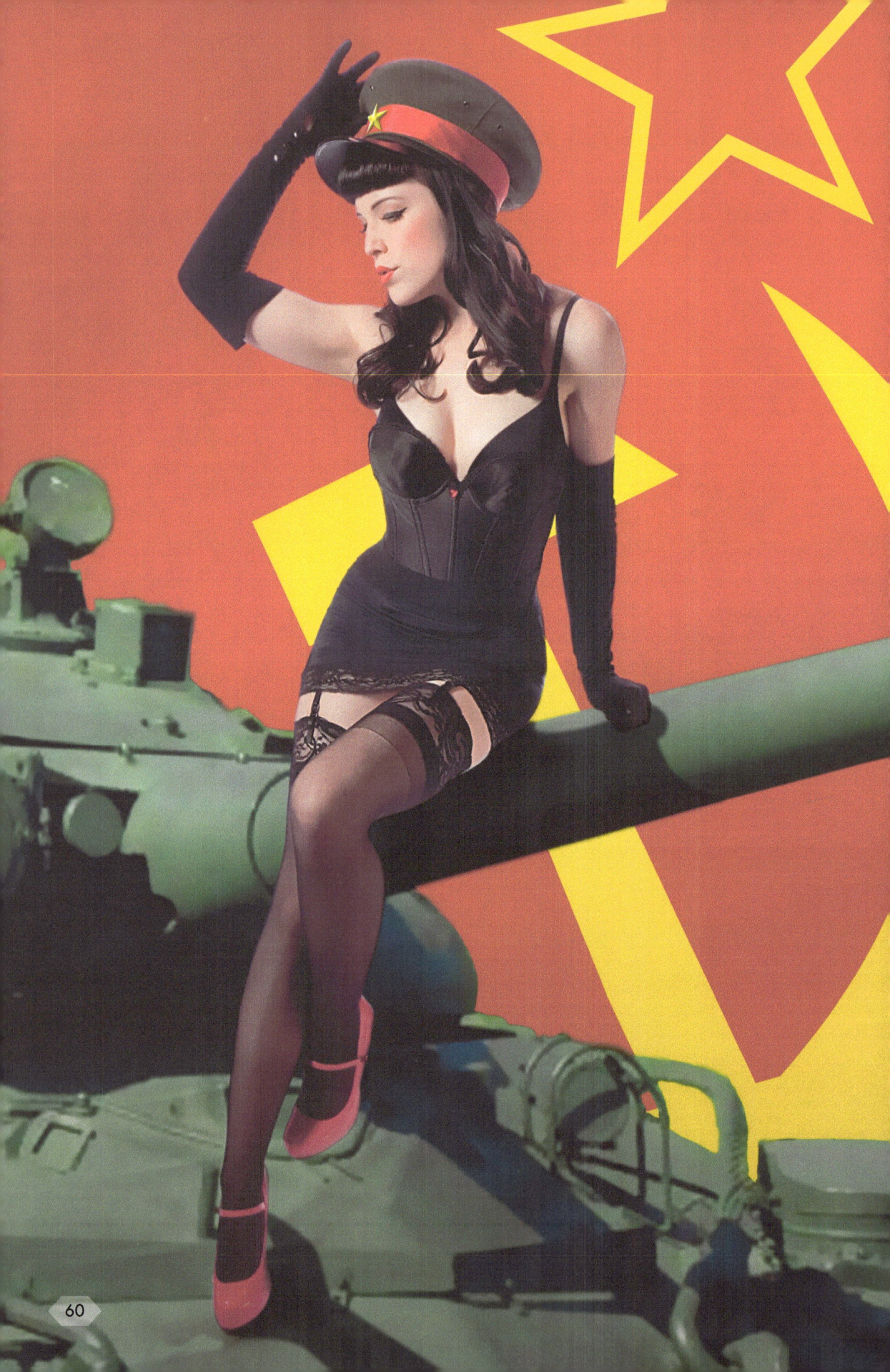

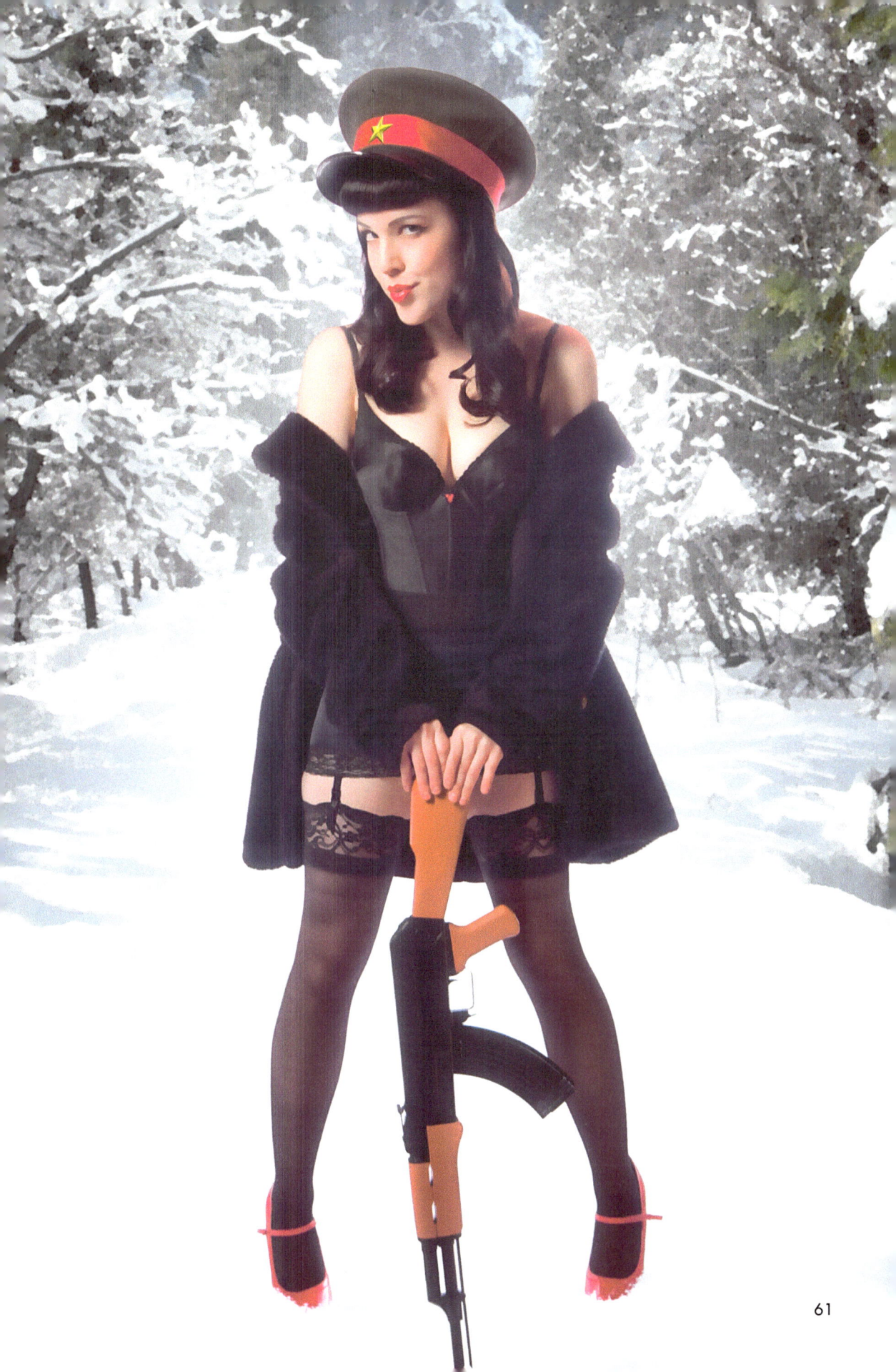

BEHIND THE SCENES

INSPIRATION
This shoot was all about the wardrobe - leather jacket and high heel boots.

EDITING
This is another military image sourced from government-released public domain photos. Editing out the model's leg took some careful adjusting, as well as determining an angle for the foot peaking out from behind the far side of the bomb.

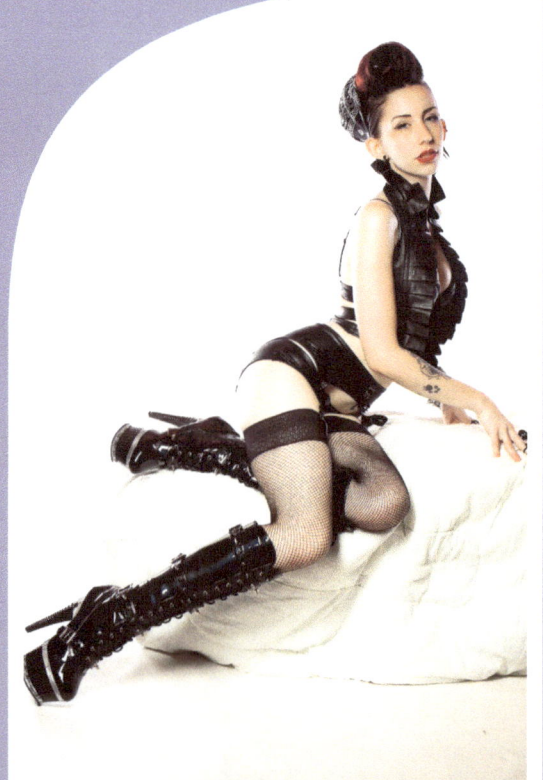

ORIGINAL PHOTO

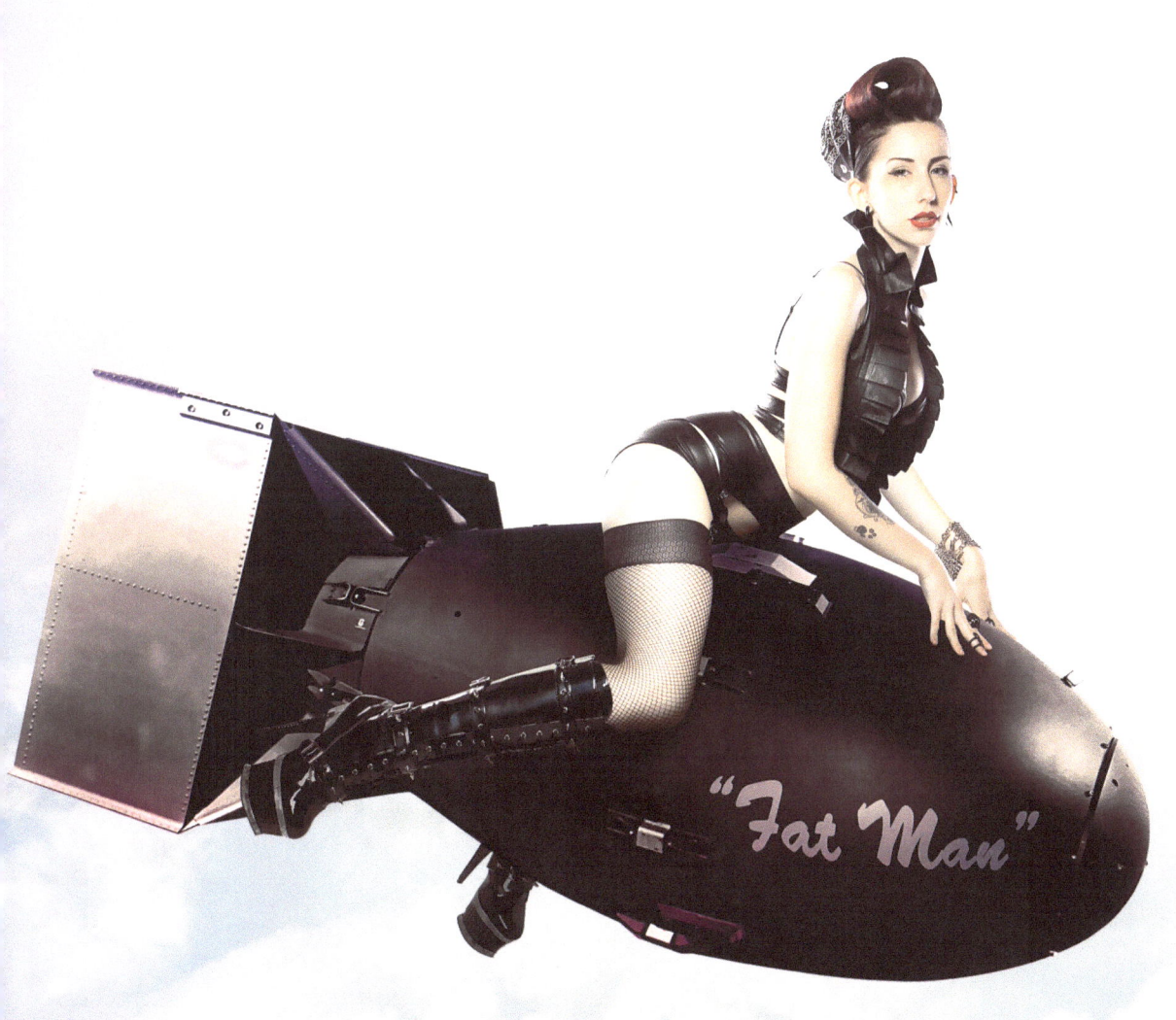

ECLECTIC THEME PINUPS

BAKING, MAD SCIENCE,
CAMP SAFARI, LIBRARIAN,
CONSTRUCTION, CARTOON
CHARACTERS, FRUIT, TROPICAL
ISLAND BEACHES, MERMAID.

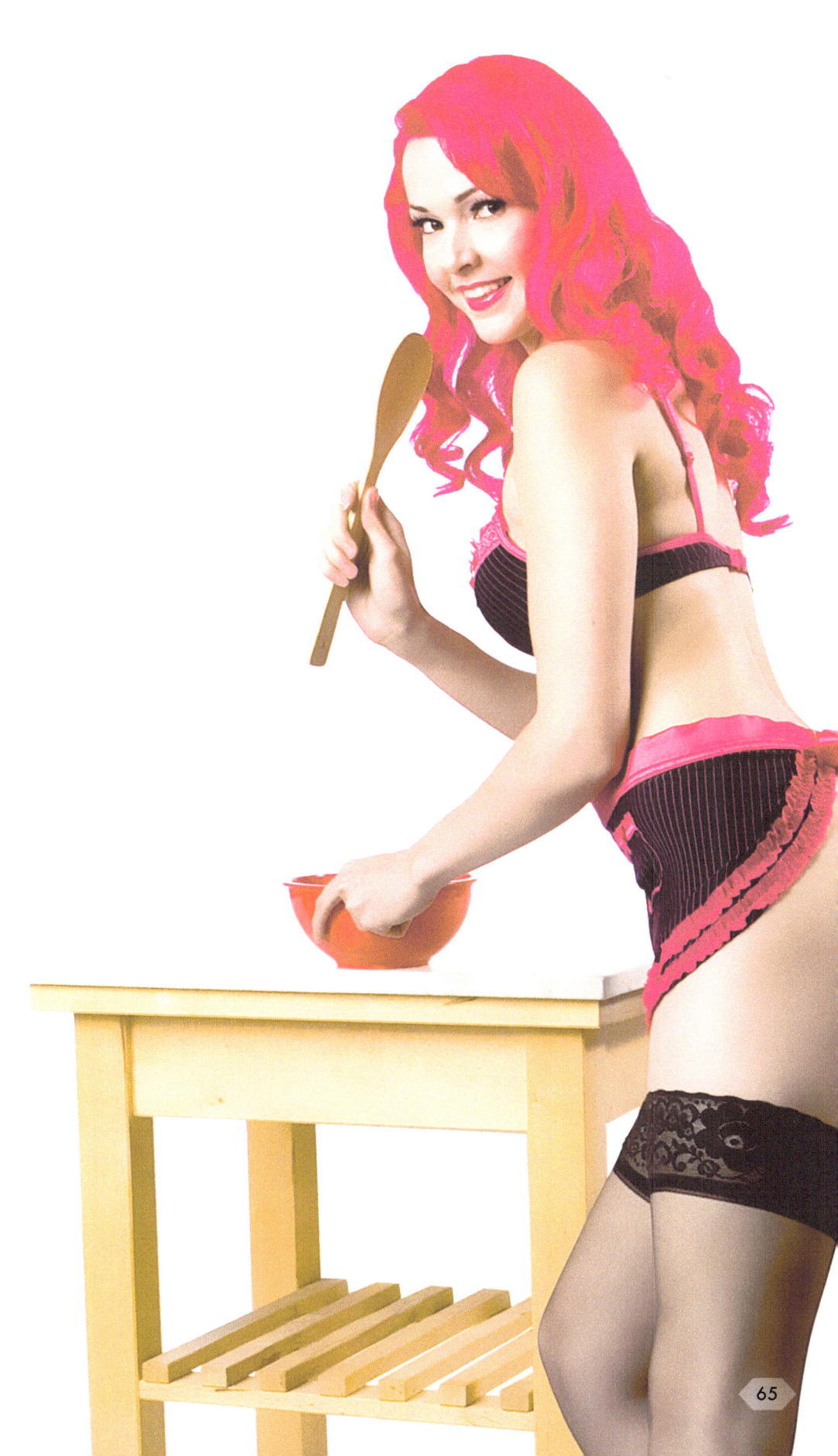

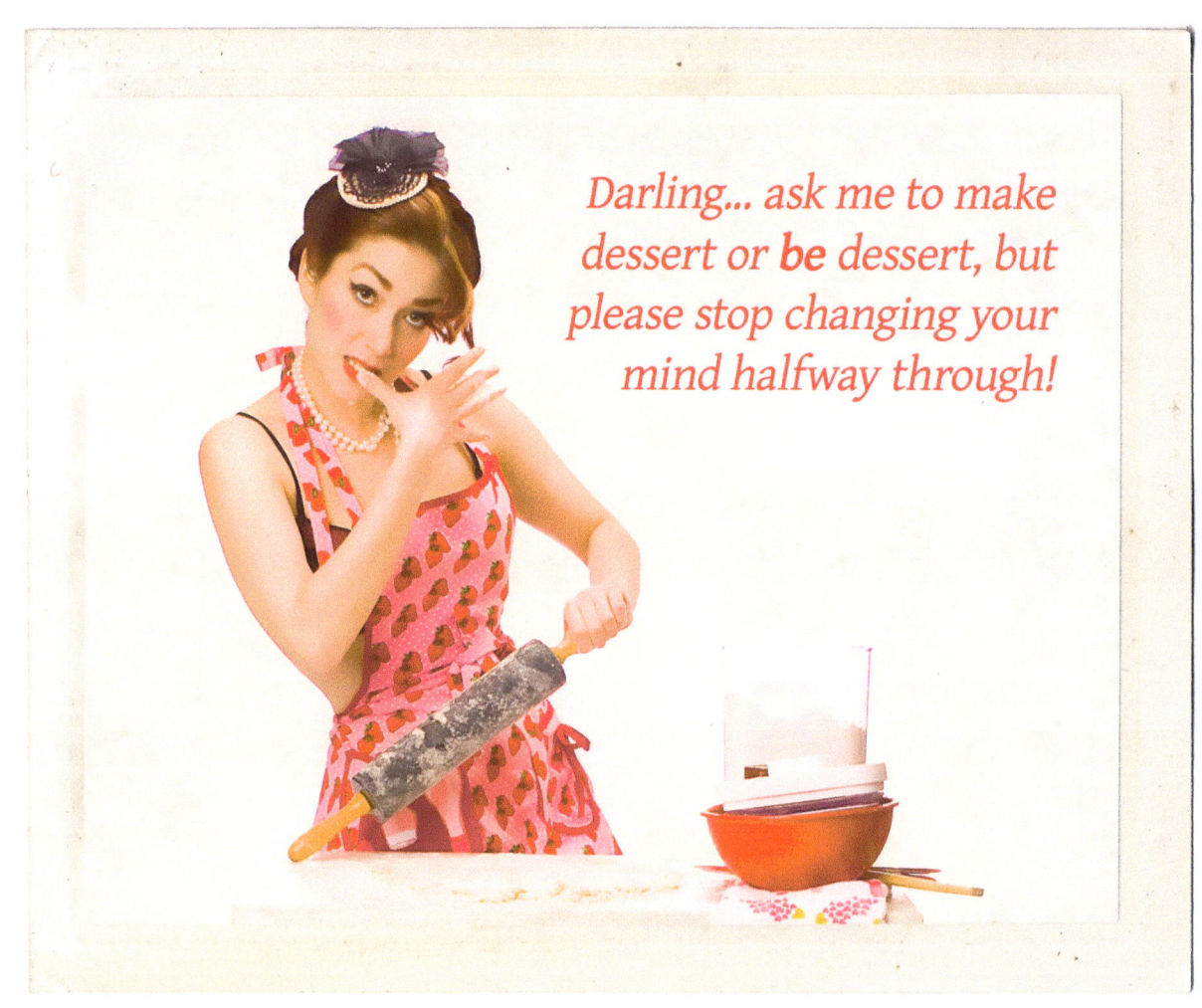

Darling... ask me to make dessert or **be** dessert, but please stop changing your mind halfway through!

Wrap your lips around something amazing!

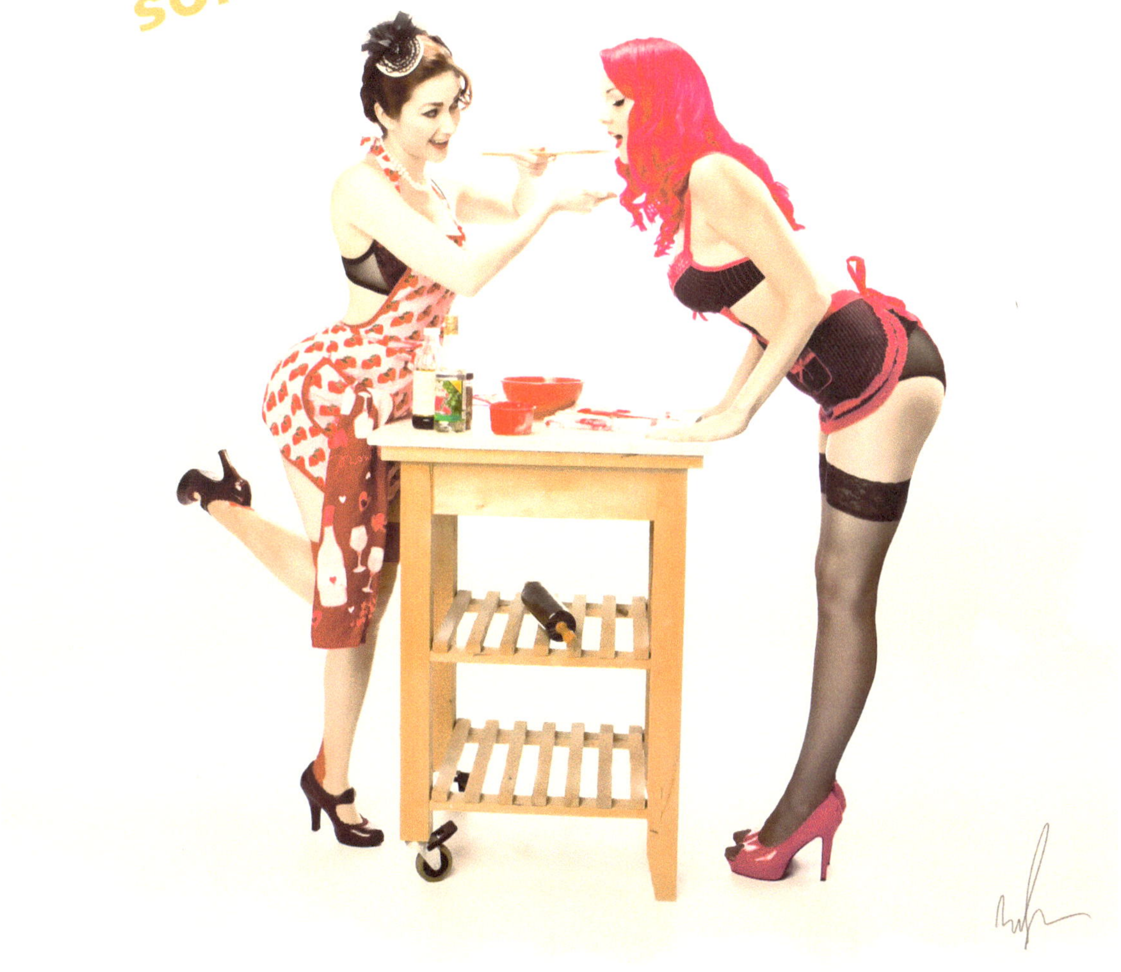

Delight your dinner guests with brave new culinary inventions or reinvigorate stale recipes with vibrant color and luxurious flavor.

In a cake, in a drink, or even on a salad, *Sherman's Syrups*® are sure to excite even the most somber tastebuds.

Don't just make it special...
Make it *Sherman*.

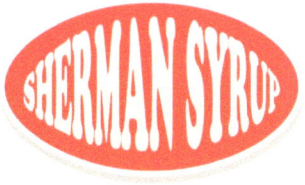

67

Well *of course* I would make an excellent model, but imagine the *scandal!*

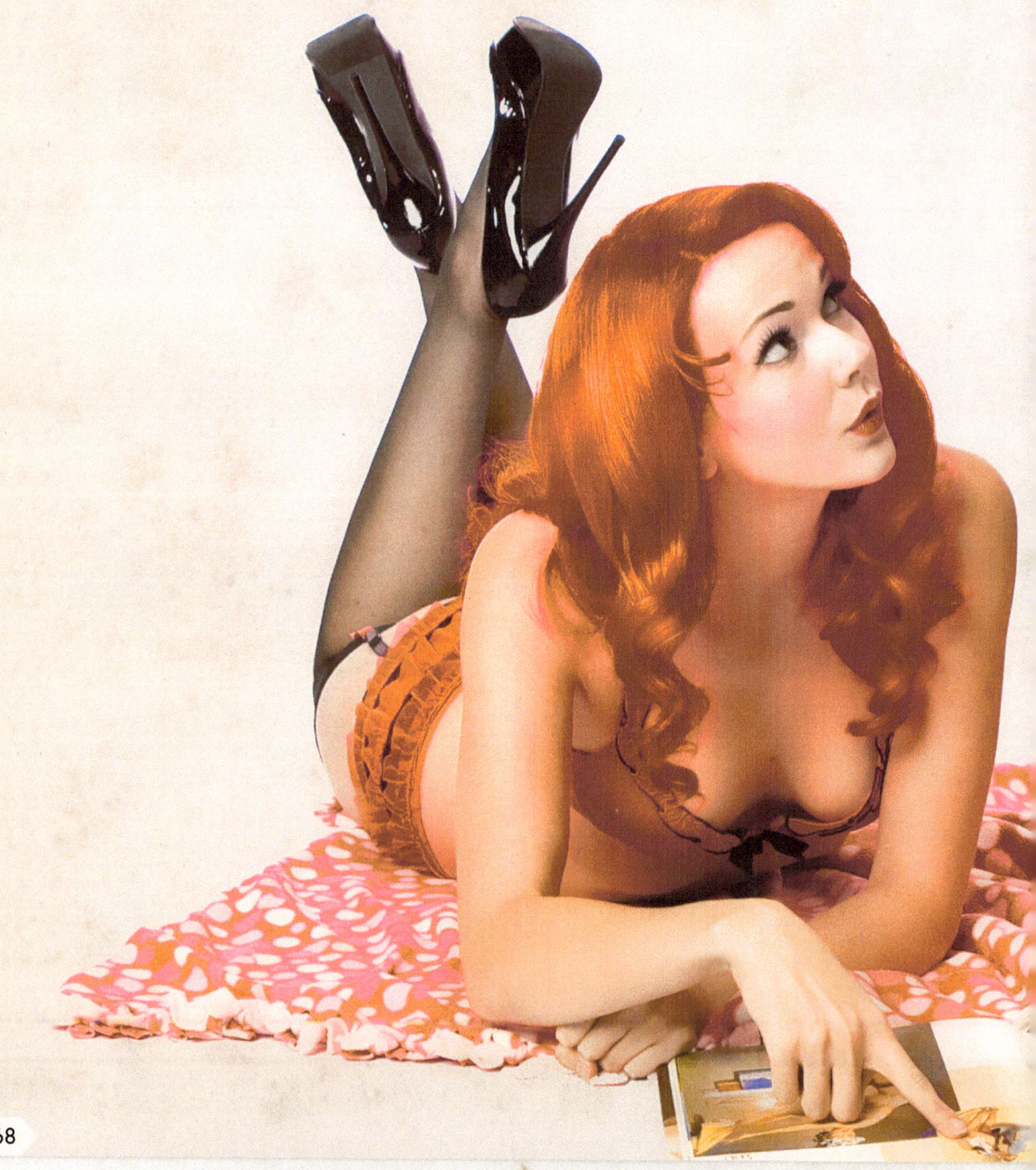

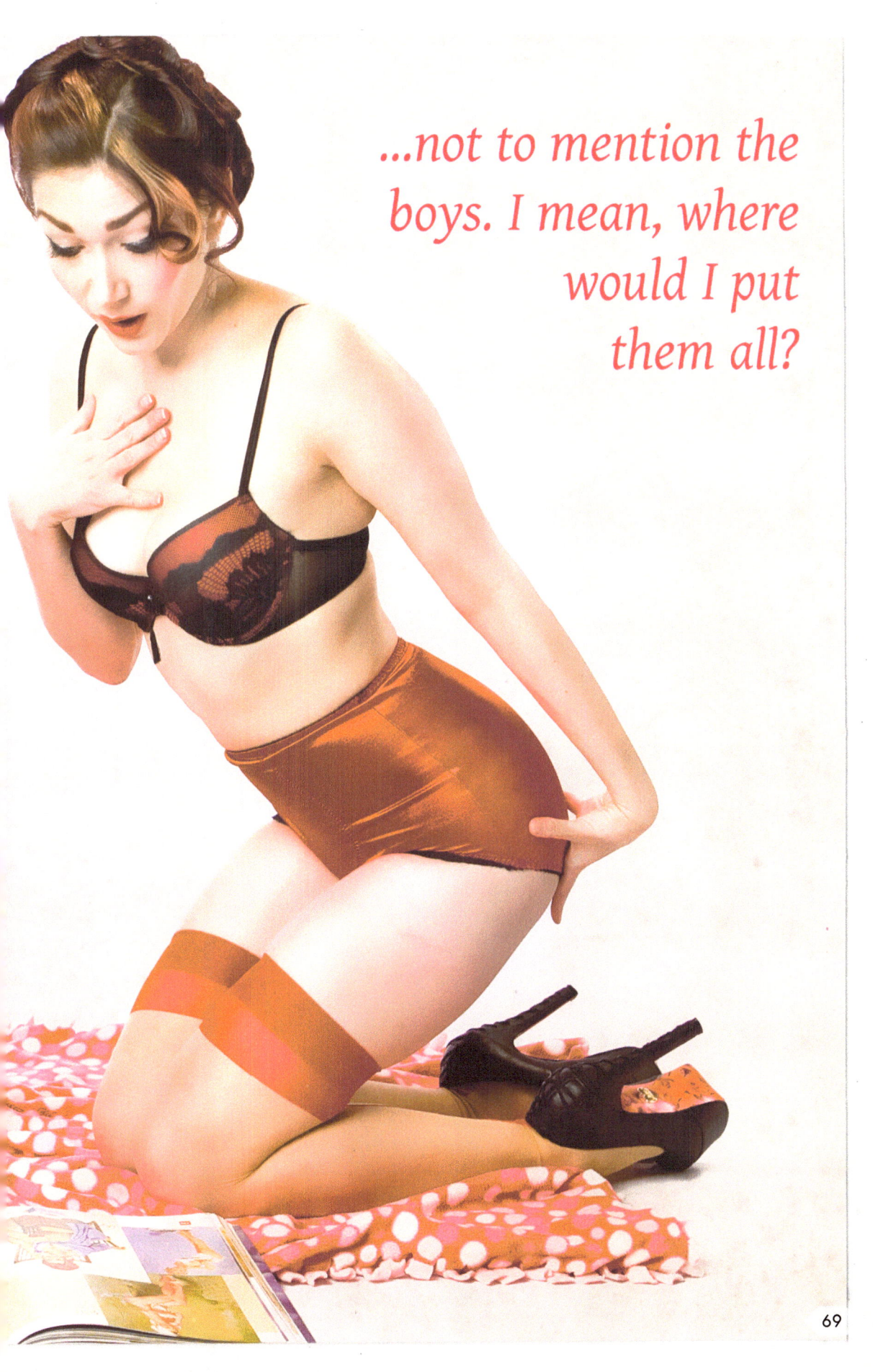

...not to mention the boys. I mean, where would I put them all?

BEHIND THE SCENES

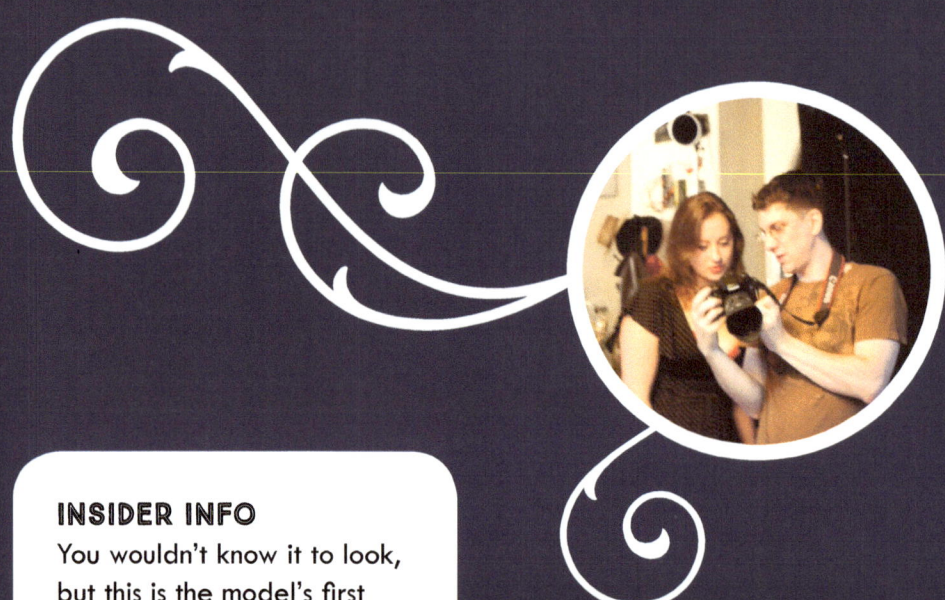

INSIDER INFO
You wouldn't know it to look, but this is the model's first time modeling.

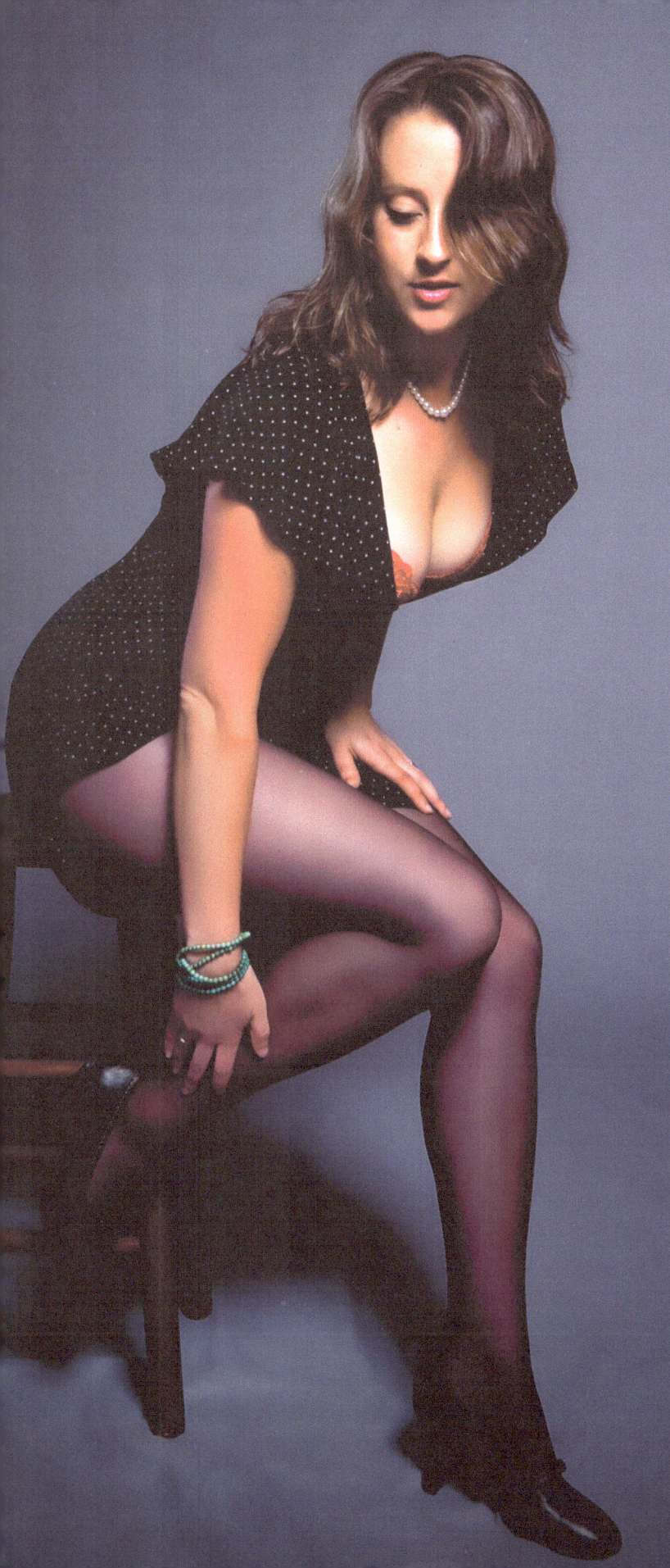

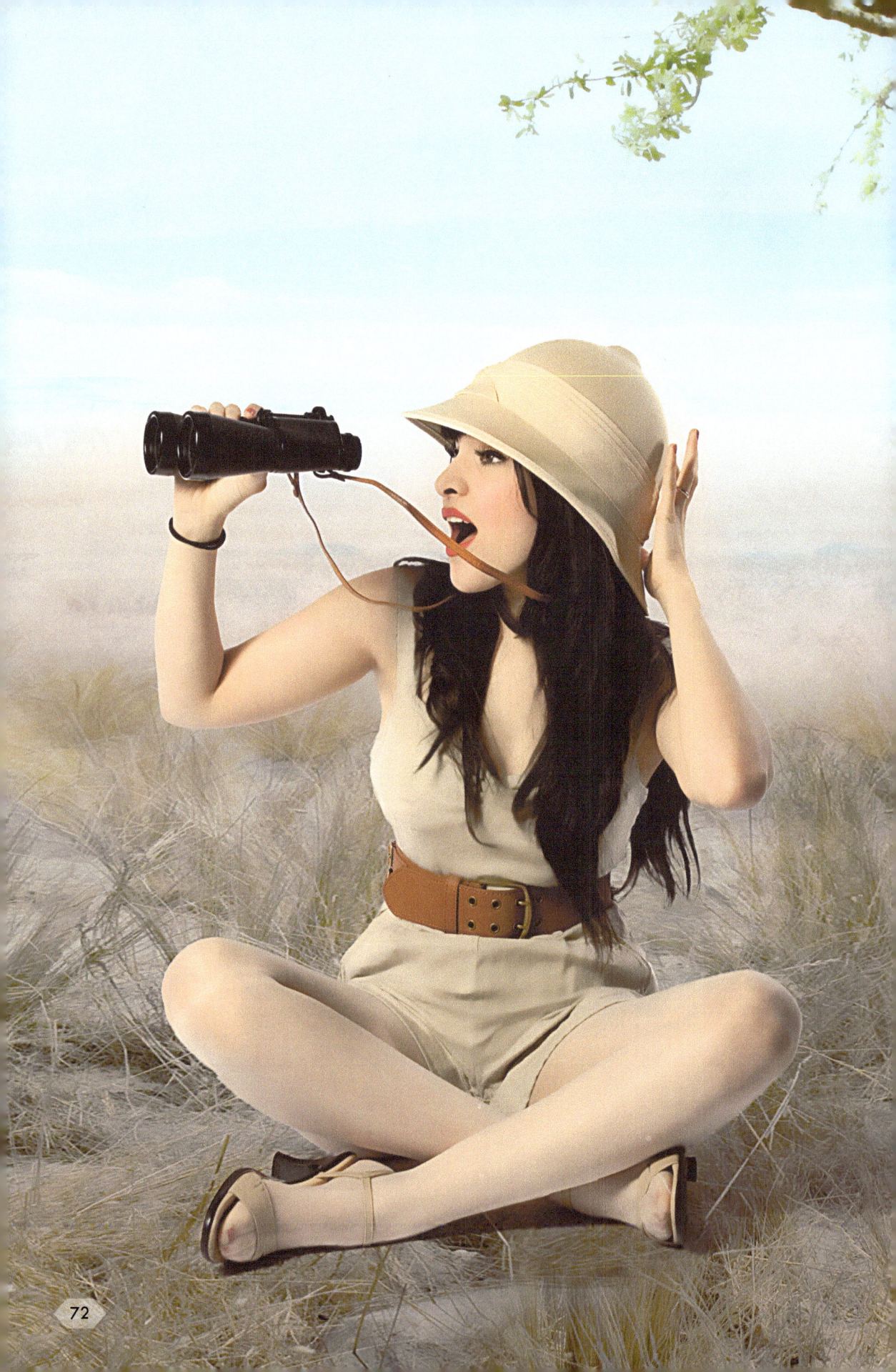

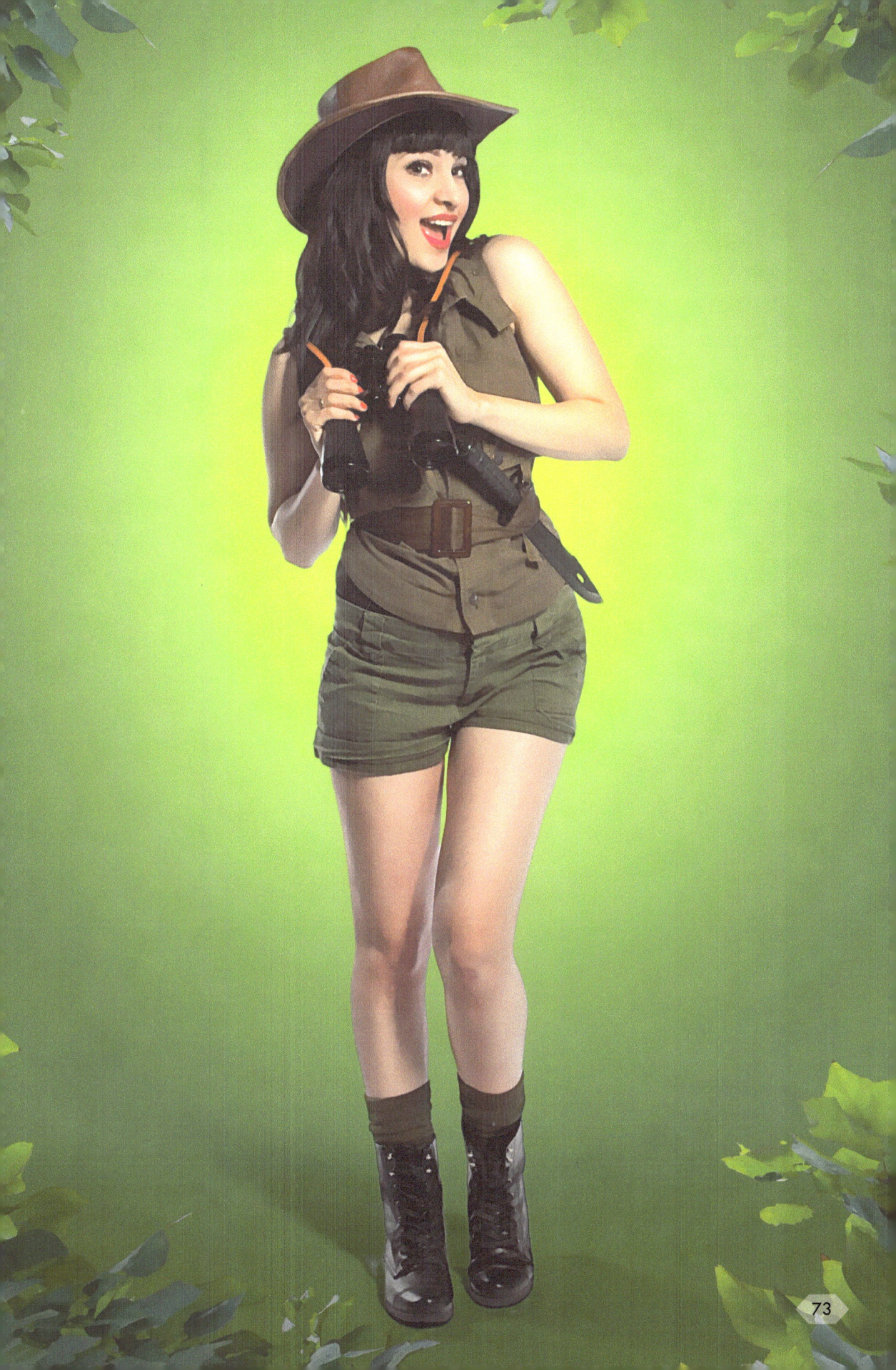

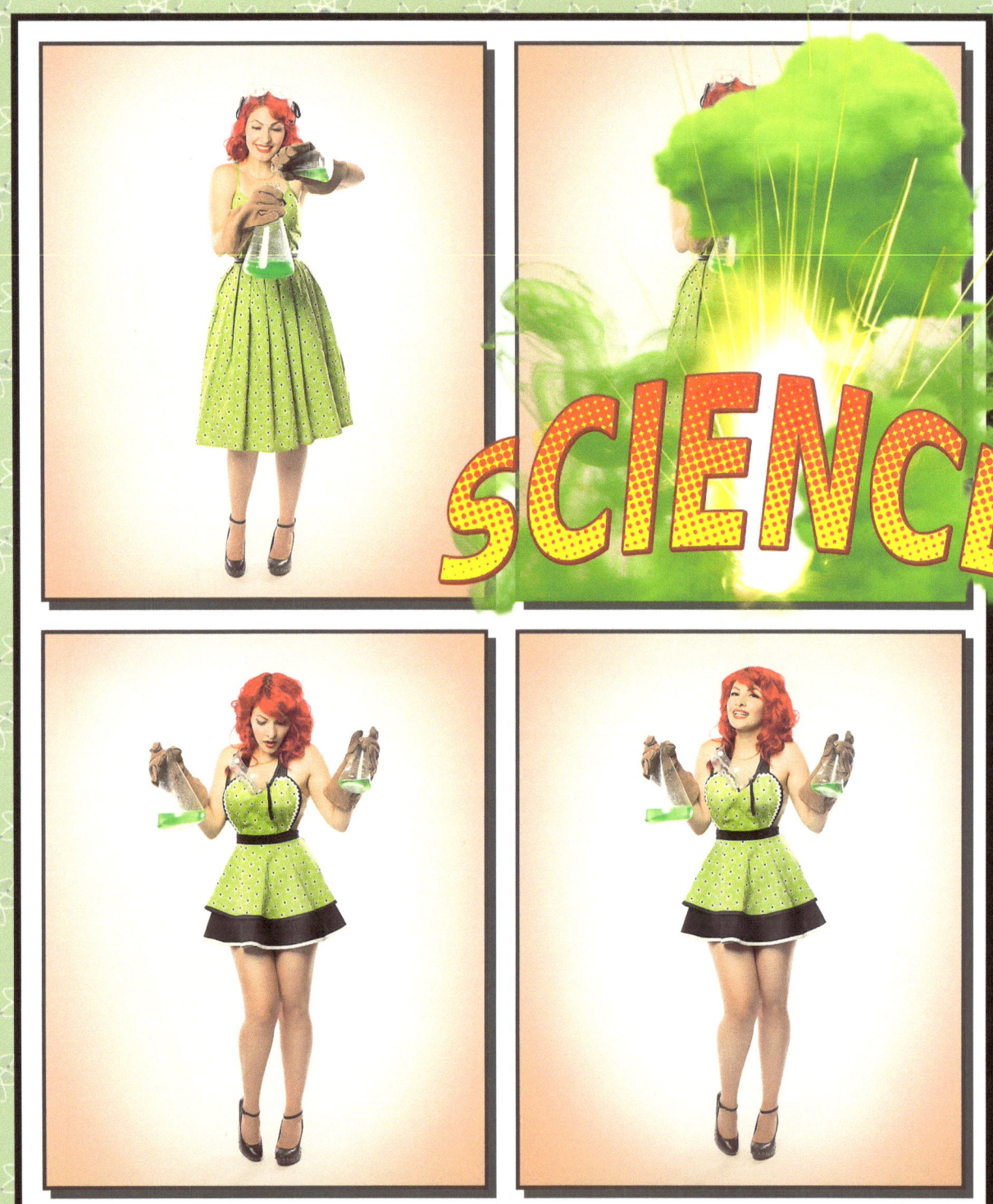

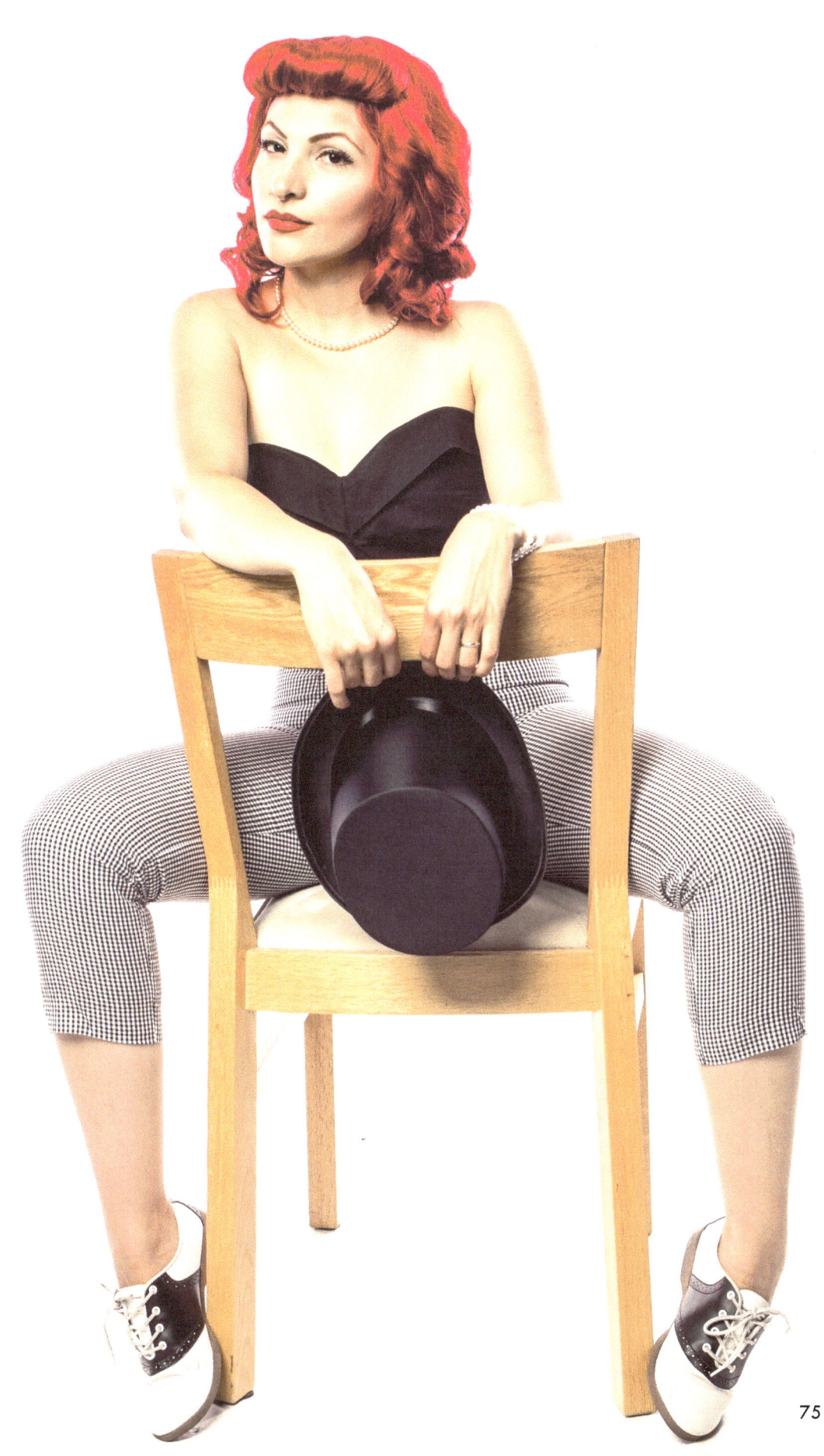

BEHIND THE SCENES

HAIR AND MAKEUP
Carefully crafted hair and makeup were an essential part of preparation for this photo shoot.

BACKGROUND
A simple white backdrop was used and then fully replaced with beach sand and scenic ocean waves.

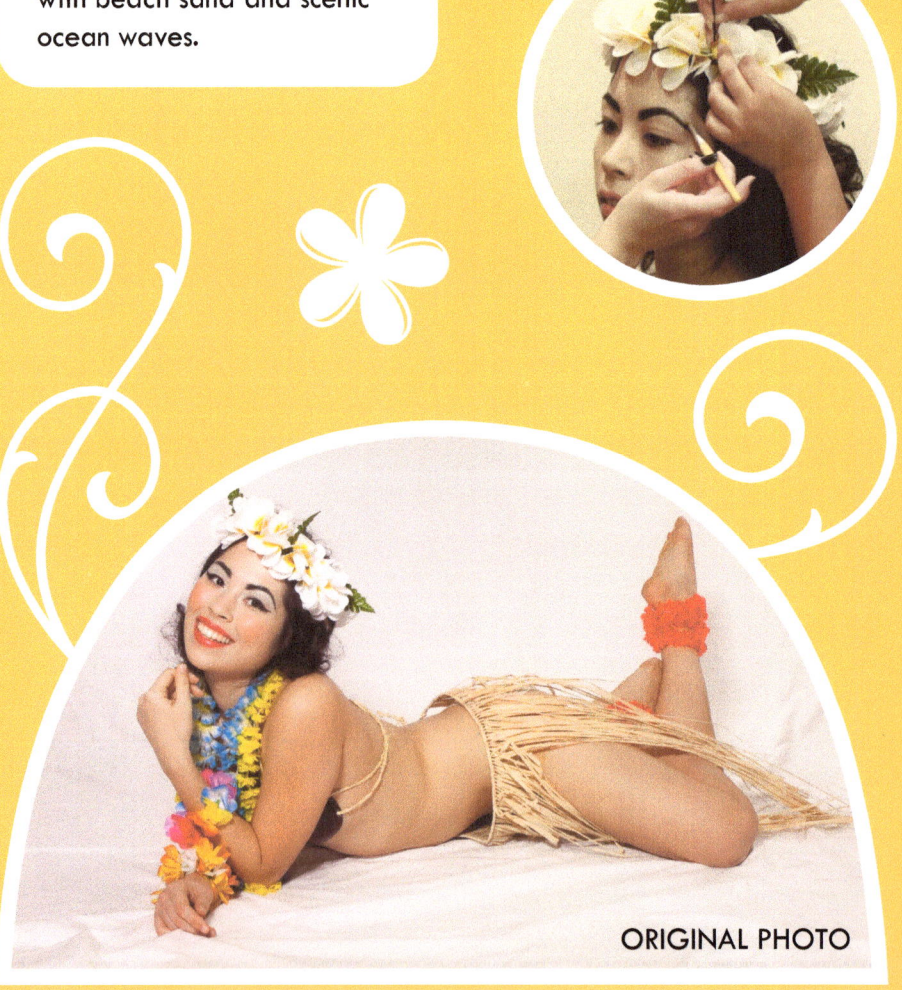

ORIGINAL PHOTO

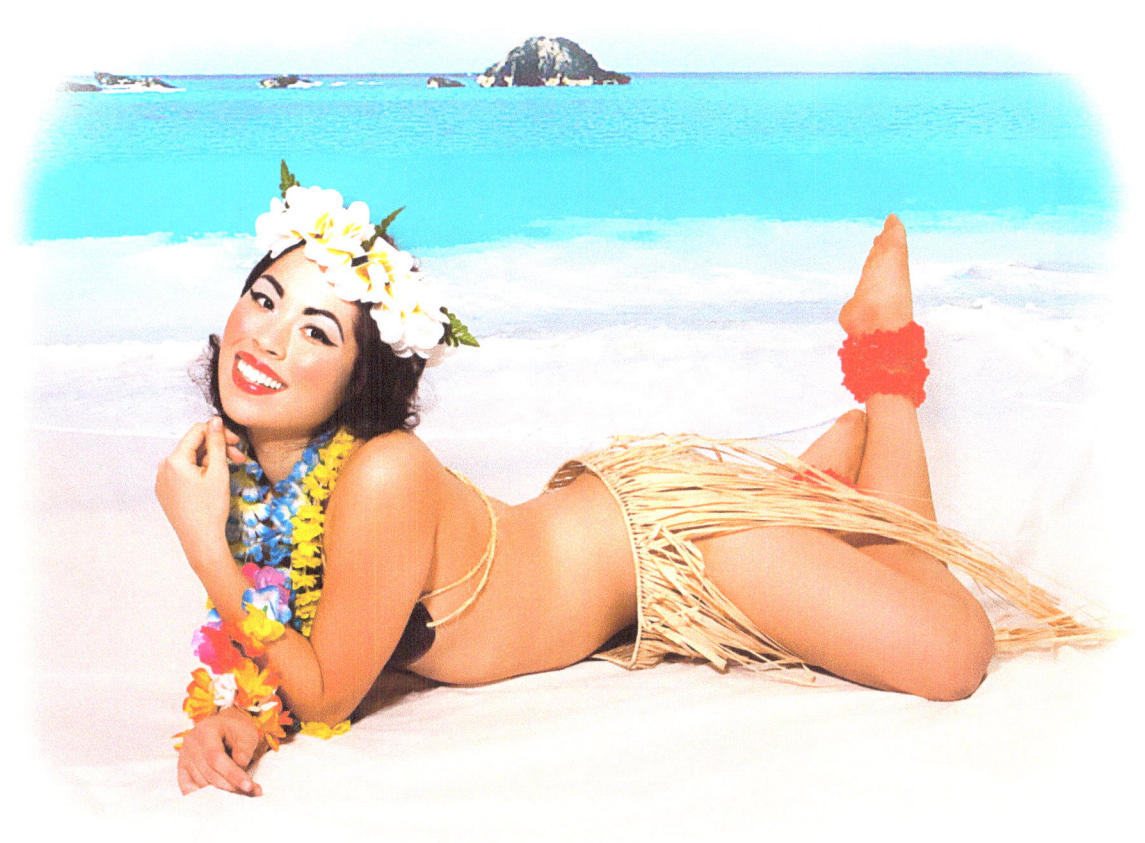

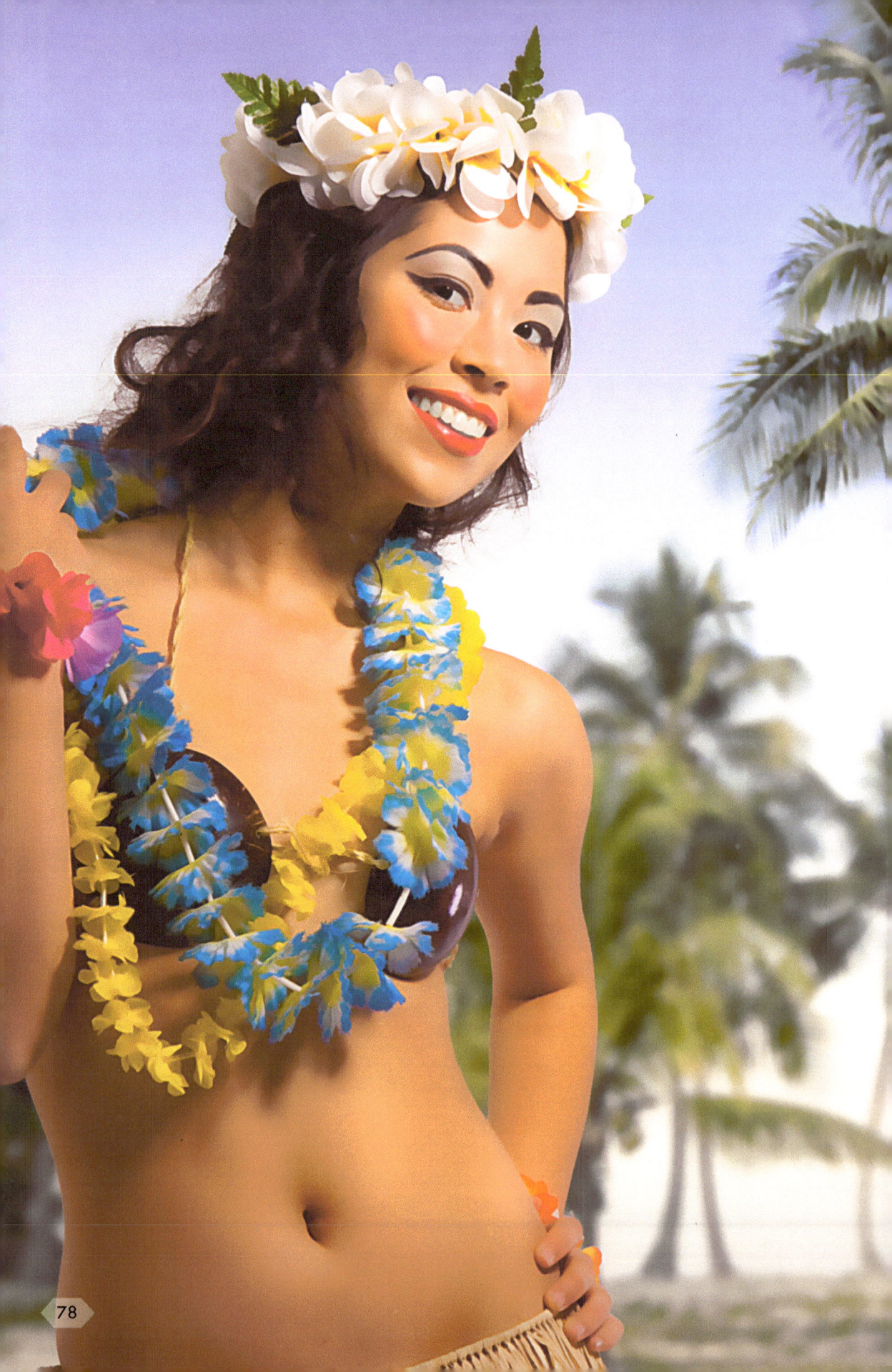

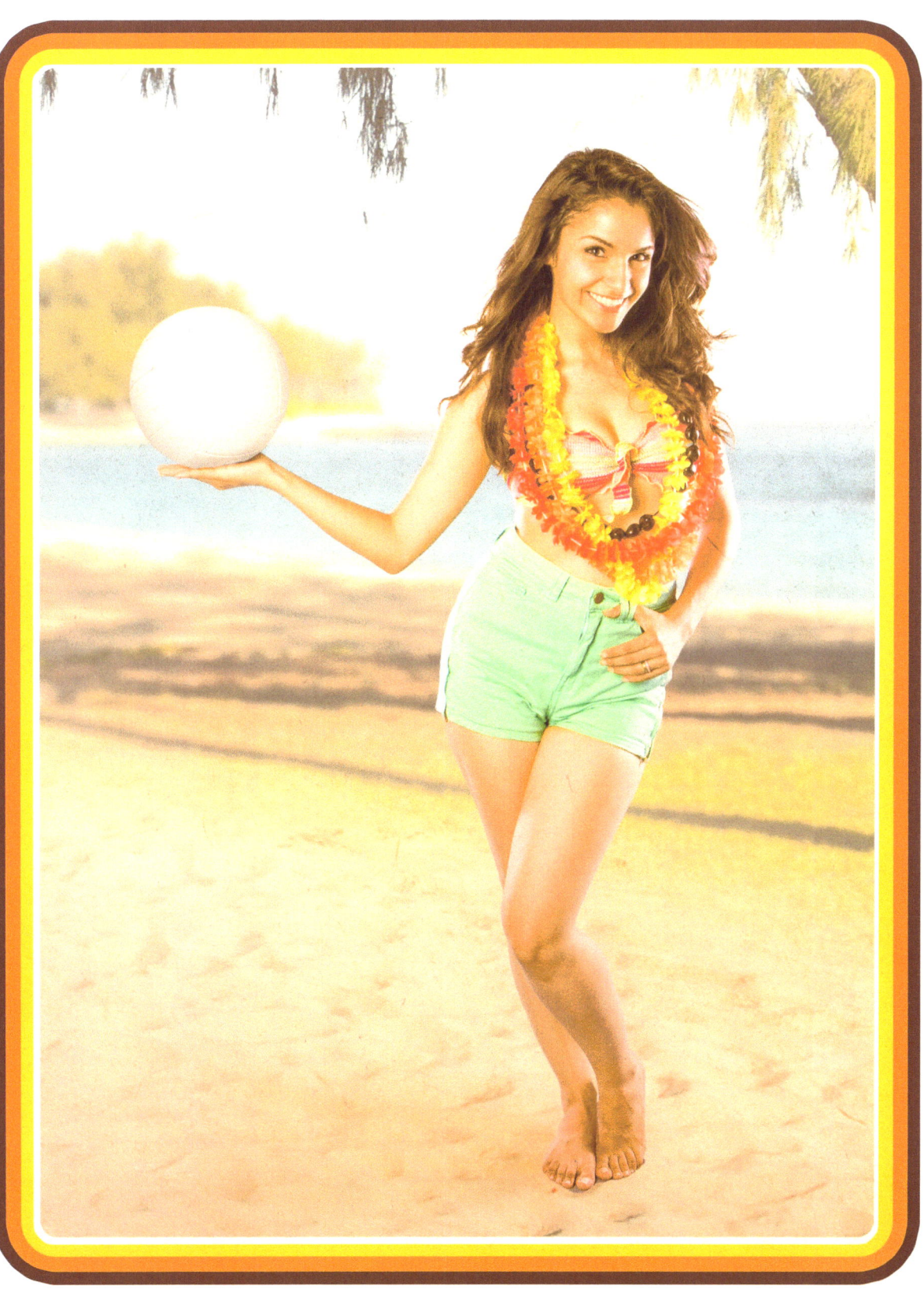

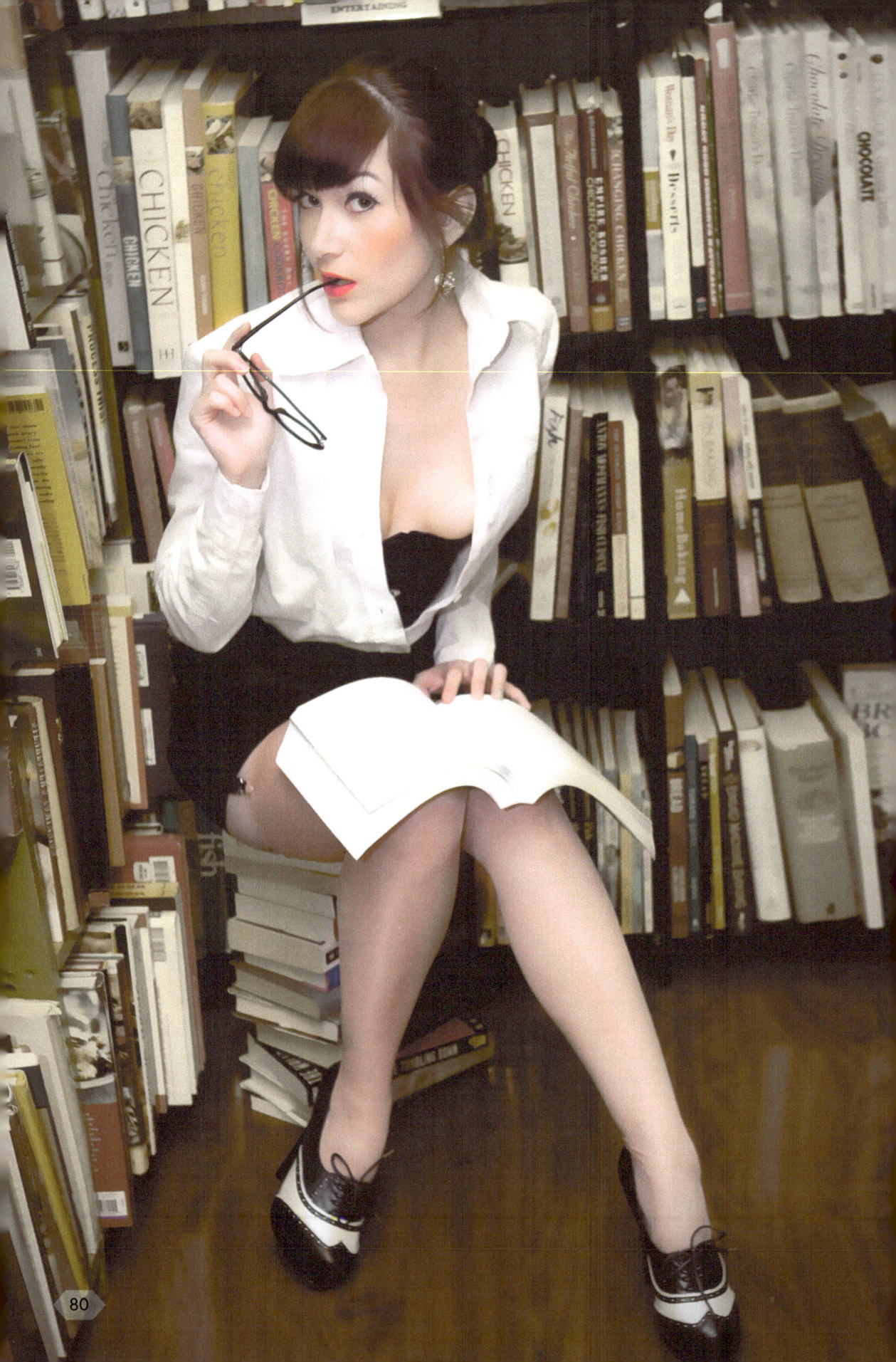

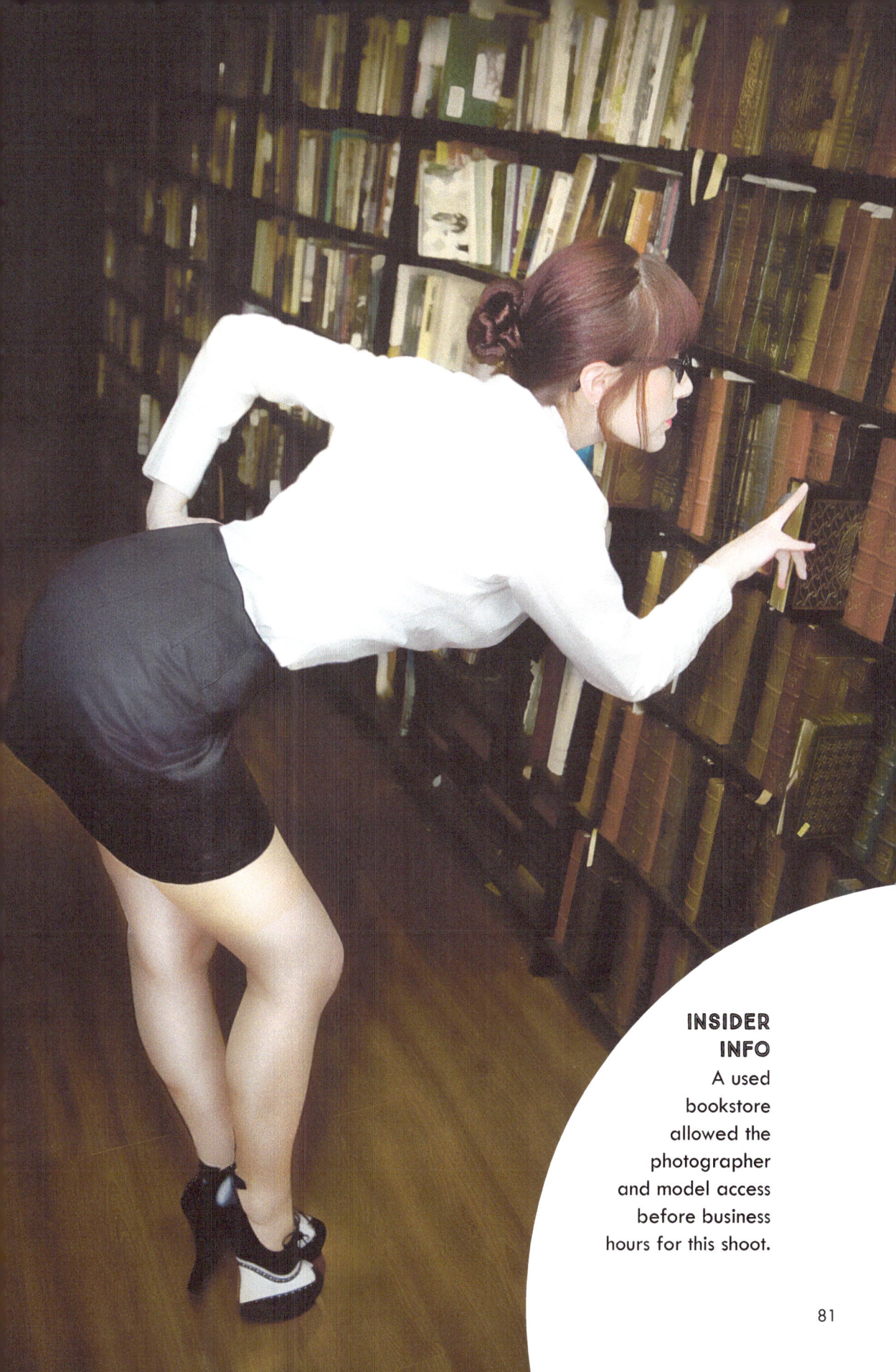

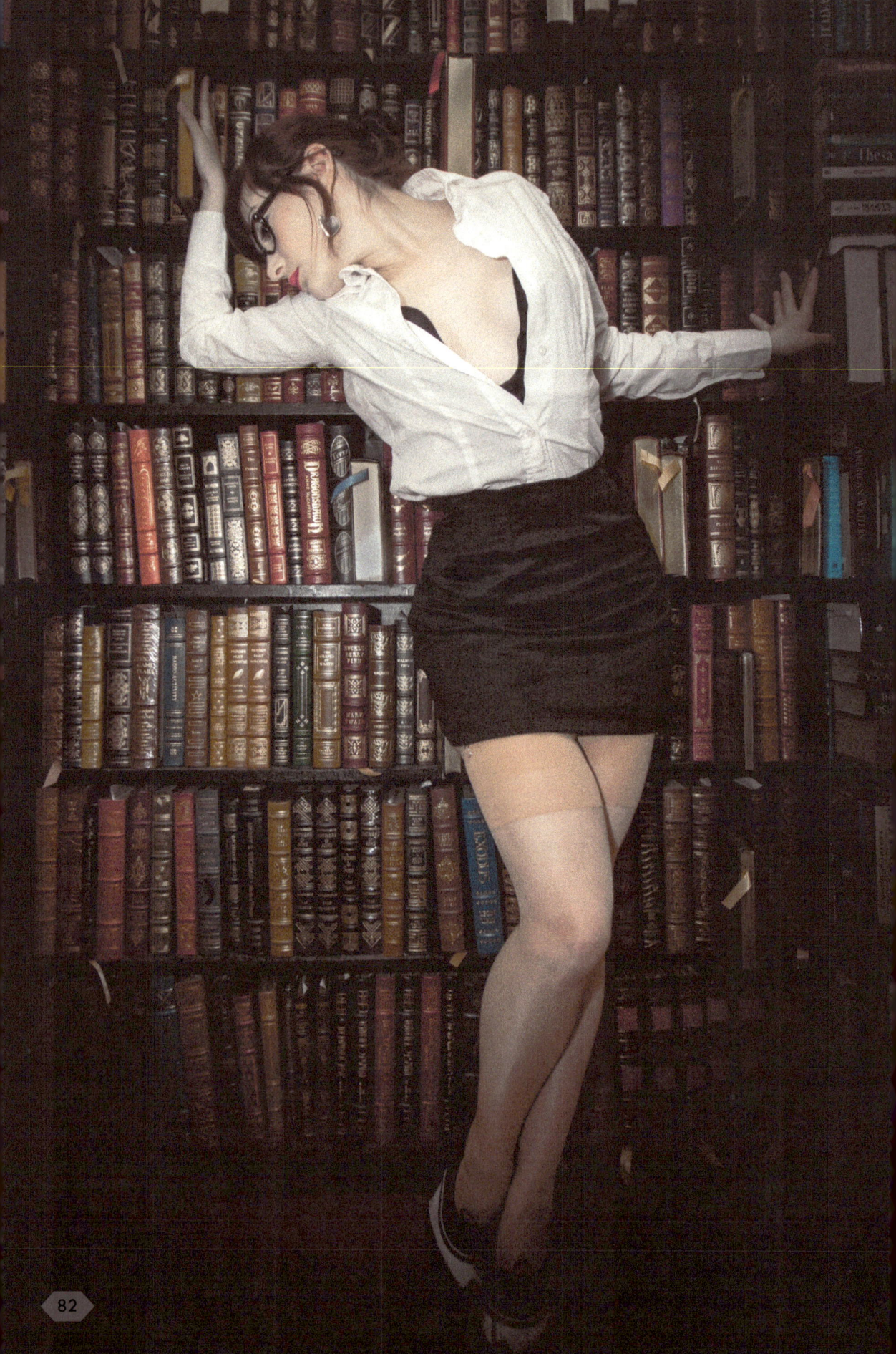

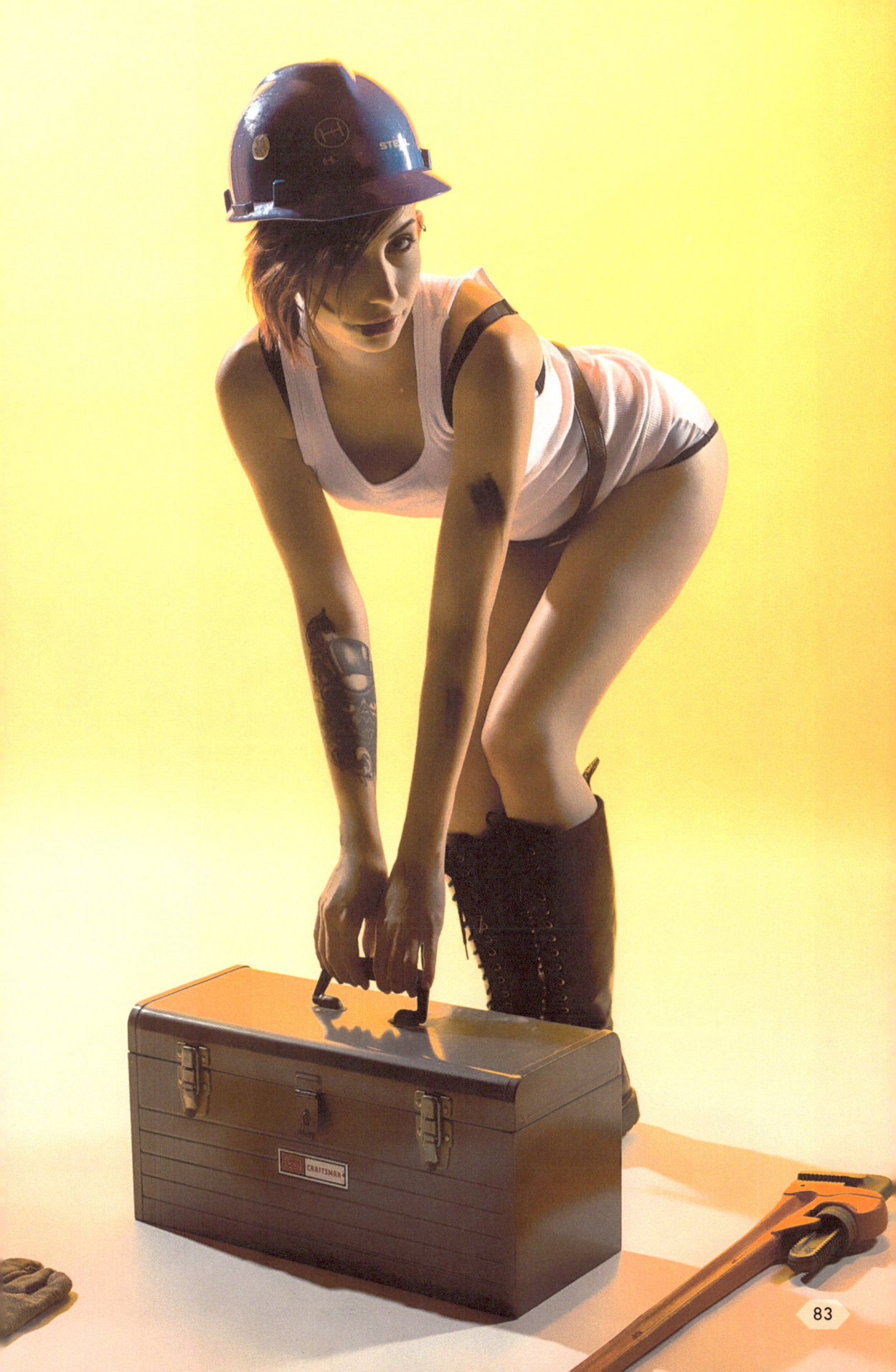

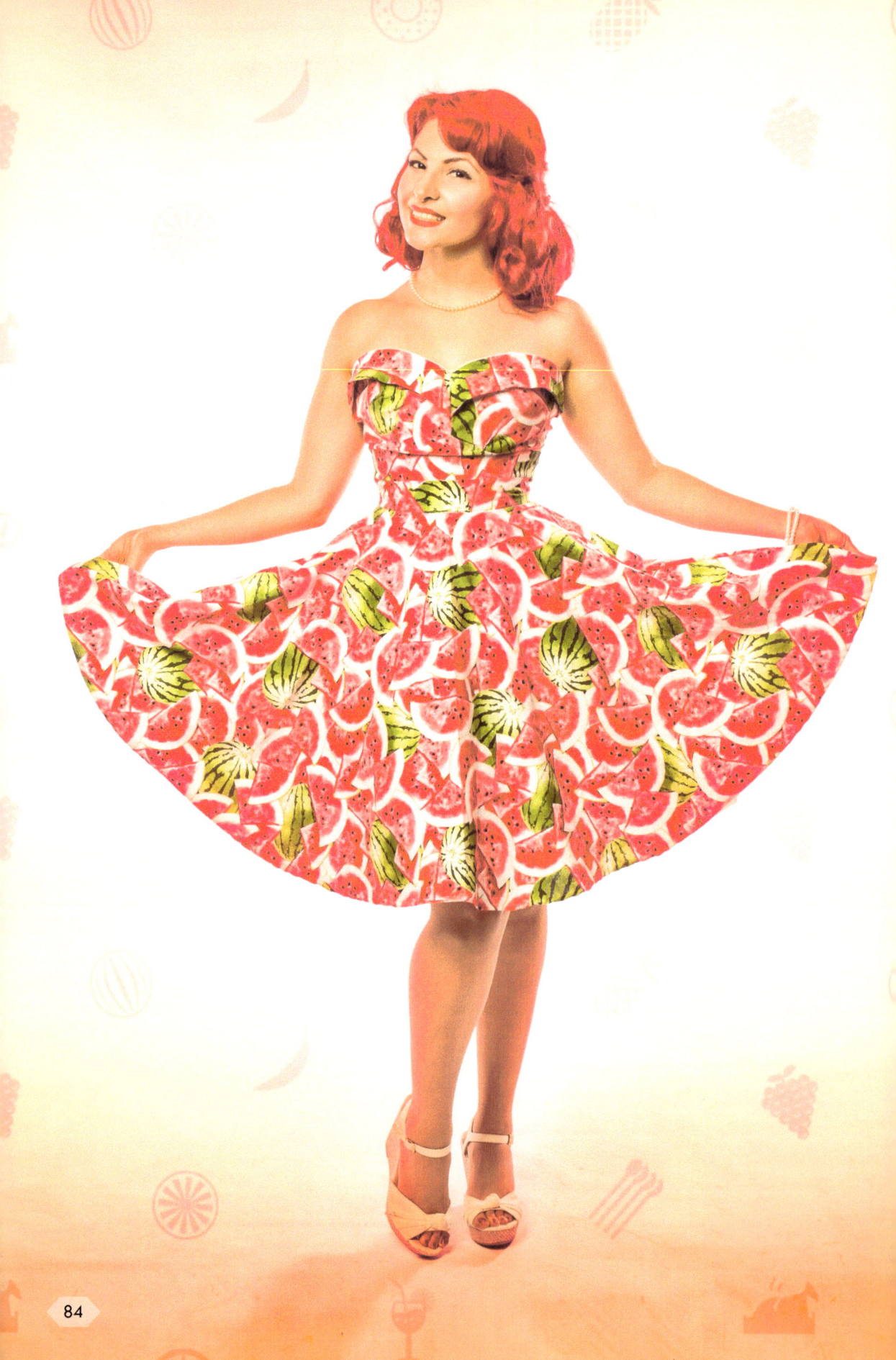

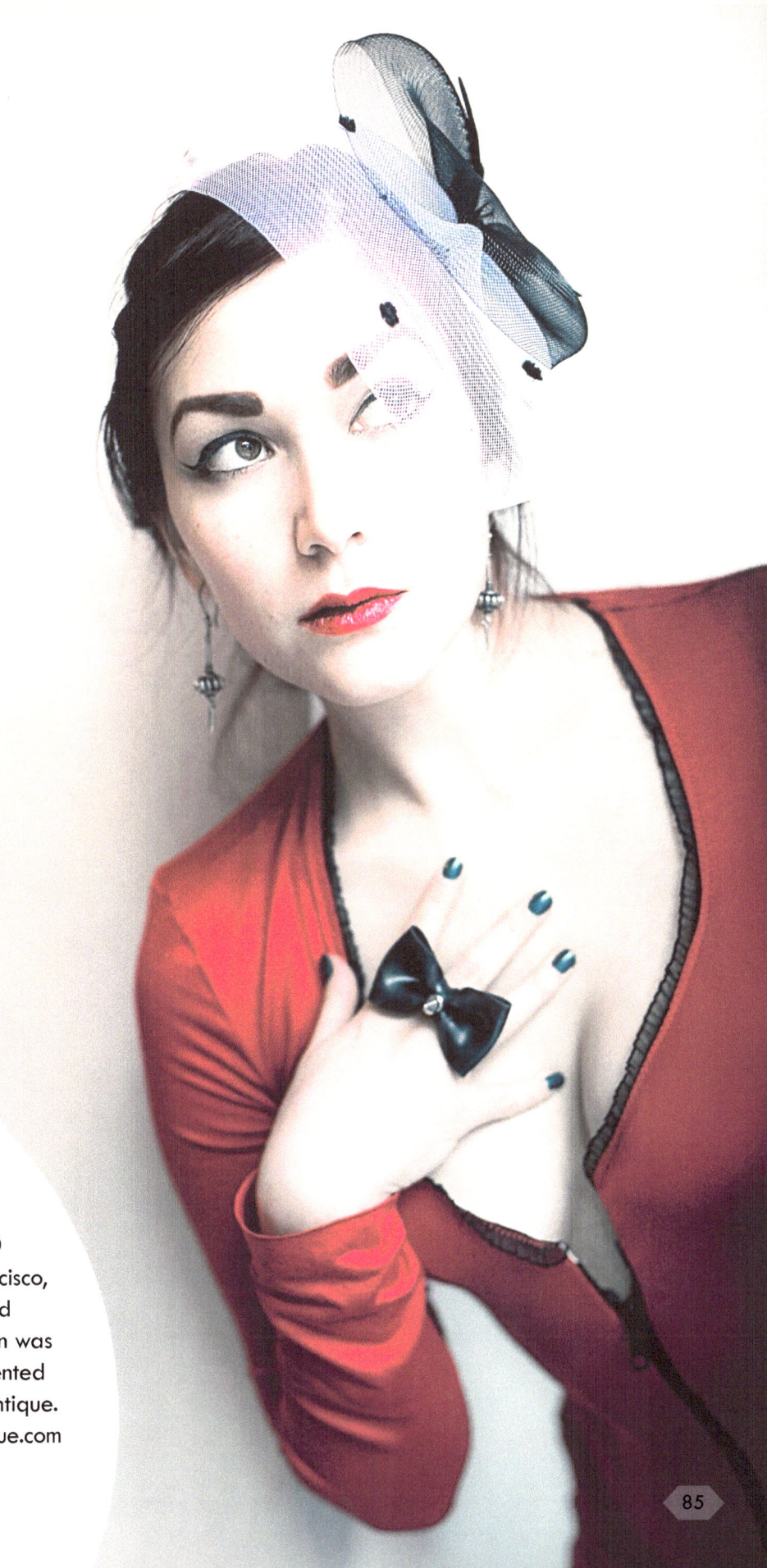

INSIDER INFO
Shot in San Francisco,
the modeling and
wardrobe design was
done by the talented
owner of Pop Antique.
http://popantique.com

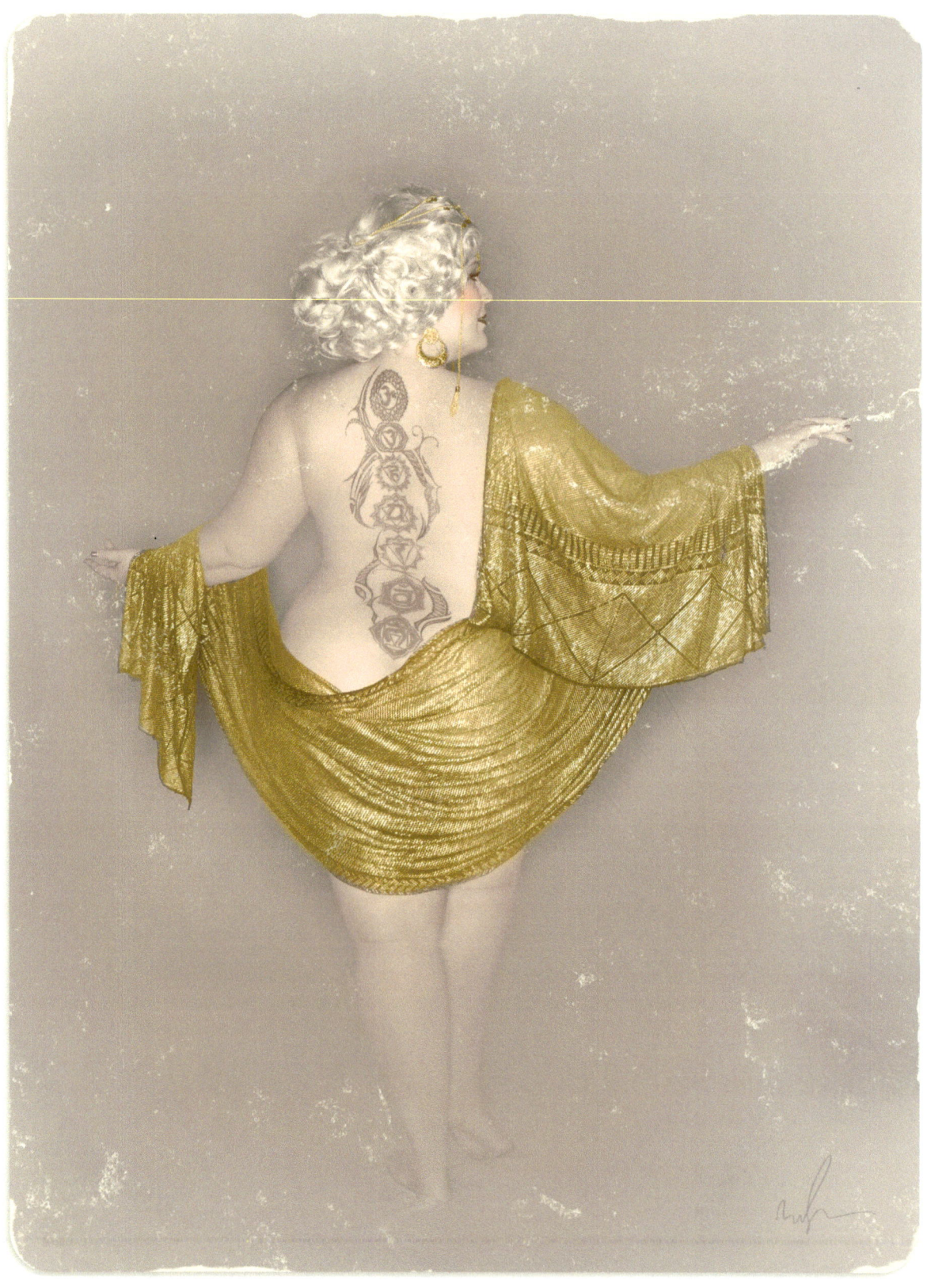

86

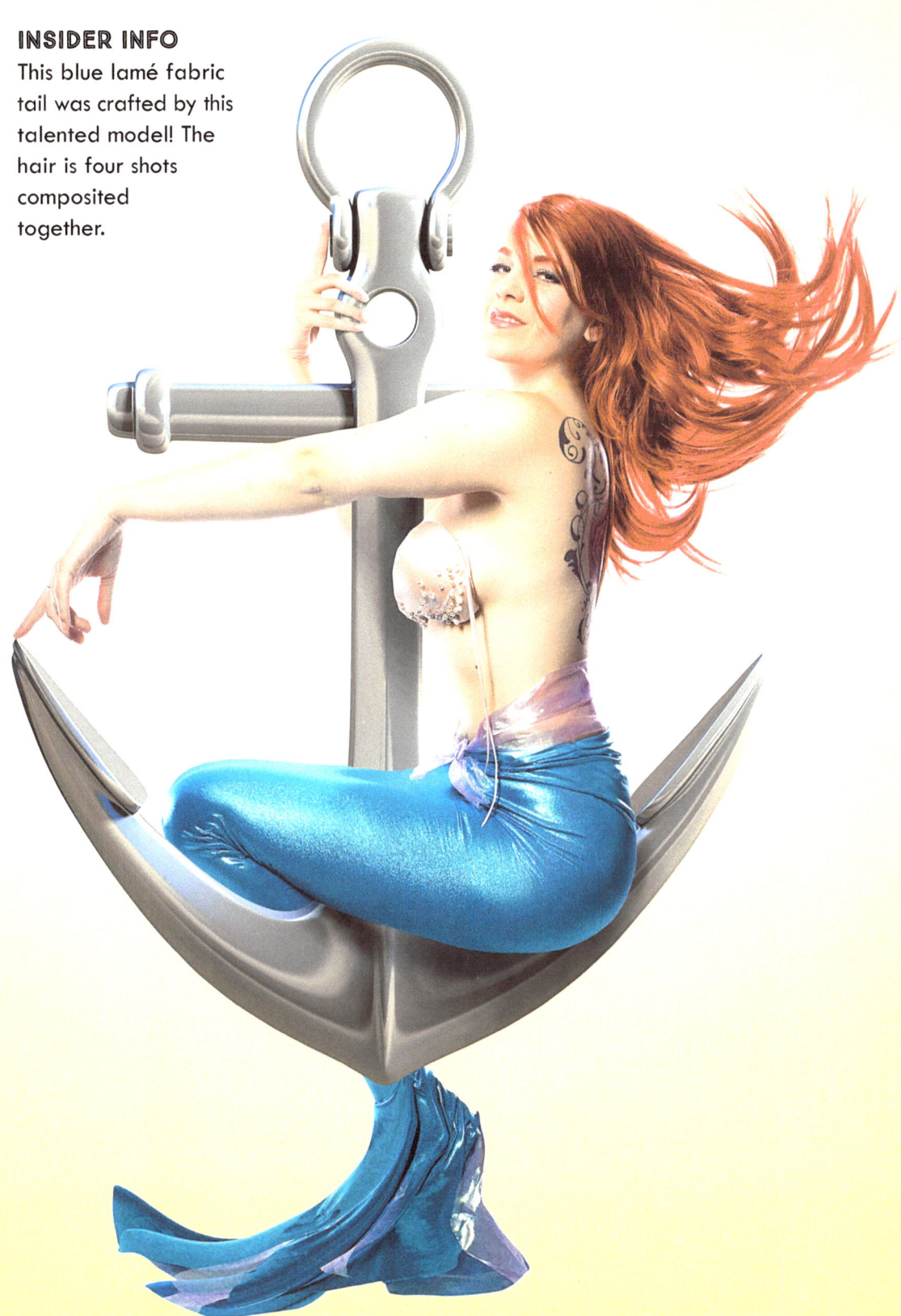

INSIDER INFO

This blue lamé fabric tail was crafted by this talented model! The hair is four shots composited together.

CREDITS

MODELS

Lavender Simone, Cover
www.modelmayhem.com/LavenderSimone

Kristina Marie, pg 7, 25, 47
www.facebook.com/kristina.marie.566148

Mz Wendy, pg 9, 11
www.modelmayhem.com/mzwendy

Victoria Dagger, pg 10, 26, 27, 66, 67, 69, 80-82, 85
www.facebook.com/myboyitsdagger

Sharon Marie, pg 13, 14, 15
www.modelmayhem.com/sharonmarie

Raven Le Faye, pg 16, 29, 37, 65, 67, 68
www.modelmayhem.com/ravenlefaye

Katherine Celio, pg 17, 21, 33
www.katherinecelio.com

Mina Caustic, pg 18, 19, 22
www.modelmayhem.com/minaa

Nicole Simone, pg 20, 24, 40, 86
www.nicole-simone.com/

Gothlet, pg 23, 28, 63, 83
www.missgothlet.com/

Poisoned Grace, pg 31, 32, 36
www.modelmayhem.com/PoisonedGrace

Shiree Collier, pg 38, 39
www.shireecollier.com/

Brittany Cervantes, pg 42-43

The Crafty Pinup, pg 48, 50-55, 72-75, 84
www.instagram.com/thecraftypinup/

Felix Zatknis, pg 56
www.facebook.com/felixzatknis/

Sophie St. Claire, pg 59, 60, 61
www.modelmayhem.com/sophiestclaire

MAKEUP ARTISTS

Wendy Tran, pg 9, 11
www.facebook.com/pages/ARTISTRY-BY-WENDY-TRAN/156236876784

Juliana Bosia, pg 10, 16, 29, 37, 71
www.modelmayhem.com/2345714

Chrysalis Rose, pg 18
www.modelmayhem.com/chrysalisrose

Cerina, pg 22
www.facebook.com/DeathProofMakeup/

Make Up by Rey, pg 34, 35, 45, 49, 77-78
www.modelmayhem.com/makeupbyrey

Shiree Collier, pg 38, 39
www.shireecollier.com/

HAIR STYLISTS

Stylist Miranda, Cover, pg 9, 11, 42, 43
www.studioglam.com/miranda/

Erin Lopez, pg 10, 16-18, 21, 23, 28, 29, 33, 36-37, 63, 65-69, 71
www.facebook.com/victoryroll

Intertwine Hair Design, pg 34, 35, 45, 49, 77, 78
www.intertwinehairdesign.com/

Shiree Collier, pg 38, 39
www.shireecollier.com/

OTHER CREDITS

Pg 10: Thank you to Park Place Vintage for providing wardrobe and costumes. www.parkplacevintage.com

Pg 20, 24: Thank you to Dark Garden for the cincher.
www.darkgarden.com

Pg 20, 24, 83: Thank you to Pop Antique for bow, wardrobe.
www.popantique.com/

Pg 84: Thank you to Davina Devine for the wardrobe.
www.facebook.com/DavinaDevine

MERCH & MEDIA

You can find Maxwell H. Johnson's pinup photography available on Society 6 - where beautiful art prints, framed art, and other products feature the pinup artwork shown in this book.

SOCIETY6 STORE:

🛍 http://society6.com/maxmakespinups

FOLLOW MAXWELL H. JOHNSON'S WORK:

📷 @MaxMakesPhotos

f http://facebook.com/maxmakesphotos

WEBSITE:

www http://maxmakesphotos.com

www.ingramcontent.com/pod-product-compliance
Lightning Source LLC
Chambersburg PA
CBHW050731180526
45159CB00003B/1189